398 DIY

Tips, Tricks and Techniques

Practical Advice for New

Home Improvement Enthusiasts

Ian Anderson MSc LCGI

HANDYCROWD MEDIA

398 DIY Tips, Tricks & Techniques

Practical Advice for New
Home Improvement Enthusiasts

Published by handycrowd media Reg No. 995979268 Norway

ISBN 978-82-93249-13-9

Disclaimer: The author has made every effort to ensure that the information in this book is accurate. However, since it cannot be determined what you intend to do with this information or how competent you are, it shall be your own responsibility to ensure this information meets your specific requirements.
The author is a professional builder educated in the UK and the working practices and observations in this book reflect this. It is your responsibility to ensure the advice given in this book is suitable for your country or situation as working practices and rules differ from country to country. It is your responsibility as the homeowner to ensure you have permission to carry out alterations and additions to your home.

Seek local professional advice if you are in any way unsure.

I'd like to dedicate this book to Ian Welby, who trusted his gut feeling about a 19-year-old stranger with little more than a trowel to his name.

CONTENTS

PREFACE

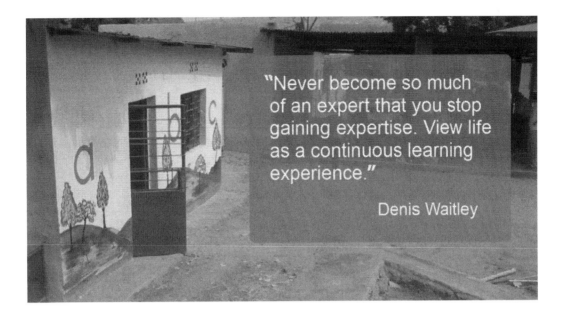

"Never become so much of an expert that you stop gaining expertise. View life as a continuous learning experience."

Denis Waitley

Over the past 35 years I've worked with many people; read countless books, articles & blog posts and during all that time, I've never found someone I couldn't learn something from. Often, it's something small but useful, or it might be something interesting or even something that's just amusing. But occasionally it's something fundamental. In those instances, I always find it mind boggling that I could get to my age and not know about this particular thing, since it appears to be common knowledge.

So here's the thing, 'you don't know, what you don't know'. And the only way to minimise the things you don't know; is to constantly expand the people you touch. Online or offline, it doesn't matter much, you're going to learn something from everyone.

Now, we're going to spend a little while together in this book, but I'm sad to say that I don't know you, or even what you're capable of. But it's my hope, as our paths cross on these pages, that I can teach you something small or maybe even something revelatory. After all we've both taken a different route to get to this point.

And if life has taught me anything at all, it's that
I'm sure you could teach me something too.

DULL BUT IMPORTANT SAFETY NOTICE

This book talks about using tools, working with electrical items, climbing on ladders, roofs, or scaffolding etc. It also talks about working with heavy or potentially dangerous materials and machines. Staying safe **must** be your **No.1 priority**. You should wear the right personal protection equipment for the job and get into the habit of working safely, every time.

Go online and seek the specific advice you need to stay safe during your planned project, the hse.gov.uk and osha.gov websites are good places to start. People are hurt every minute of every day, whether it is you or not, is your choice.

I don't want to hear you hurt yourself because you did something reckless or dumb, because then I'd feel bad and you don't want that. Always take your time, be careful and for goodness sake use your common sense, because if it scares you, or feels unsafe or dangerous... it probably is!

So be careful, this stuff can hurt... a lot...

INTRODUCTION

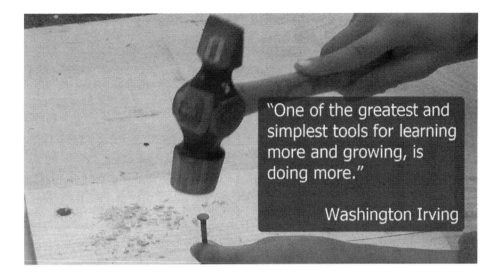

"One of the greatest and simplest tools for learning more and growing, is doing more."

Washington Irving

I've been saving tips and tricks and otherwise useful nuggets of information for decades now. Occasionally scribbled down in my notebook, but more often it's just rattling around in my head somewhere. Time now to let them loose into the world and see if they can help anyone else. Most of it I've learned on the job, either working alongside folks of all abilities or even, dare I say it, by making my own mistakes.

So welcome to my mental brain dump, and like all brainstorming sessions, it's a bit of a mix, and an eclectic one at that. I did try to categorize the list, I really did, but I know it still feels a bit random. Nevertheless, they're all real tips and advice taken from real live situations on real jobs. Did I mention it was real? Yup.

You can of course choose to read the book from cover to cover wearing your comfy pink pyjamas in your favourite armchair, or you could cherry pick, sitting on the toilet (eww!). Either way, I hope you'll use these tips as a starting point and put into practice what you learn.

A Note About Stuff

I like the word stuff. It covers a lot of, well, erm.......stuff! Because this book isn't a step-by-step guide, I'll refer to lots of things as simply 'stuff.' Just replace the word 'stuff' with tap washer, toaster, tractor or whatever else you're working on beginning with 'T'

BUILDING UP YOUR GENERAL DIY KNOWLEDGE

Let's start right at the beginning...

"Never neglect an opportunity for self-improvement."

Sir William Jones

1. But I'm Just Not Seeing It!

Take another look. No, no don't give me *that* look! I mean put your 'prejudices' aside for a moment and take a really, really, really proper look.

Because eighty percent of what we learn is visual. Remember how you can never get things back into the box they came in? That's because you forgot to notice how everything was arranged in your excitement to get at the contents.

Even the simplest of observations will teach you something about material or function if you let it. But it requires a little effort to do this, because your brain is a super computer with filters. By default, your clever brain cherry picks the things you're interested in and throws them in front of you like roadkill; and pretty much ignores everything else. (I know, shocking, isn't it?).

2. Rewire Your Brain (and no, it doesn't hurt)

It's easy. Just change your brains mental algorithm and re-write your internal code; i.e. remind yourself to notice the stuff you're using. In other words, fine tune your mental radar. I'm sure you'll recognise the scenario where you've bought something new, a car for example, and then you start seeing them everywhere? That's your radar working; those cars were there before, but your brain ignored them because you weren't looking for them. See, easy.

3. Disengage Your Autopilot

And keep it switched off (not if you're an actual pilot in your day job though, obviously...).

Instead, make extra effort to pay particular attention to the things you normally do without much thought (your autopilot). From putting more paper in the photocopier to driving your car, start noticing details.

This gets you thinking about the way your everyday things work: Look out for motion or movement, leverage, force, power, and alignment; especially how it relates to your body or how it's used.

4. It's all in the Details

To supercharge the above three points, look very closely at the small details in, on or under the things you use.

Look to see how stuff physically holds together; look for joins, fasteners, fixings, holes, gaps, slots, dimples, indentations, or casting seams etc. Look to see which bits don't move or flex a little, because that might indicate a hidden fastener of some kind.

Wonder how the above things relate to what's holding different parts together, a seam indicates a join for example. This might help you figure out how they might come apart if you need to go inside one day.

5. What if I Don't Understand the Details?

Add them together. Observe everything critically. If something stops working, look for anomalies, missing parts, burnt areas or broken parts. Look for stuff which appears out of place. Is anything disconnected, a lever or wire only fastened one end for example?

Can you see any obvious place where a dislocated part should go? If there's a free wire floating around, can you see where it might have come from (logic dictates it to be within an arc of its own length)? Are drive belts tight, (twist them through 90°)?

Look for loose screws or bolts or even an empty hole which might indicate a missing fastener. Look for illogical stuff, things which are definitely not supposed to be there; dirt, stones, corrosion, hair, sticky drinks (think remote controls), mice in engine bays etc...

If it needs particular things to work, are they present and in the correct quantities? Think about electricity, fuel, sparks, air, lubrication etc.

One thing on its own might not be enough information, try to tie stuff together to build your understanding.

6. Isn't Colour Just Decoration?

Often not, from the colour of the milk bottle top for your tea, to the antifreeze in your car, colours make great identifiers. Green means go, on or 'all clear' and red means off, stop or danger. Wire or cable colours (mostly red or brown is live, and often blue is neutral, green, and yellow is almost always earth or ground etc.).

Wall plugs. Brown is 7mm, red is 6mm, yellow is 5mm etc. (varies from place to place and manufacturer to manufacturer though).

Bagged products in the store will have a colour theme to make picking the right ones out largely a sub-conscious effort.

And oh, a lot of this colour stuff is pretty subliminal, you might not have been noticing it before now...

Marketers use this technique all the time to promote trust and brand loyalty...

7. But Change is Good, Right?

Change may be good for you, but apart from an antique developing a bit of patina maybe, it's usually a problem for your stuff.

Honing your observation skills will enable you to notice and register how things look, sound, and feel when everything is okay.

Knowing how stuff is when it's good, will alert you to when things change, (hardly ever good in this context). This is useful because stuff rarely fails without displaying some kind of symptom, however small.

These often-tiny changes are advance warnings, which might help you diagnose a problem before something fails completely (i.e. so don't ignore them!).

8. But I Still Can't See Anything

As designs get ever more complex, not everything is obvious or clear. Often there is hidden stuff or multiple things happening.

Don't expect some things to give up their secrets easily; you might have to try a little probing, pulling, flexing, and poking.

Sometimes nothing is obvious, you just can't see what it is you're looking at. So eliminate the things you know are not a problem, and eventually, as Sherlock Holmes used to say, "when you have eliminated the impossible, whatever remains, however improbable, must be the truth".

9. What Else Will Help Me to See Properly?

Obvious I know but I'll say it anyway; never struggle in poor lighting conditions, you'll miss something important. It's amazing how much better it is to work in good light. Treat yourself to some good light sources: e.g. LED stick lamp, head torch, regular torch and even flood lights on tall stands if you can afford them.

10. What if I Always Forget Stuff?

Part of observation is remembering what you've seen and learned; so, whenever you're looking at something, remember to make notes or take snapshots (phones are brilliant for this) to help you understand and remember it all, especially if the job will take several days or if you expect delays.

It's amazing how easy it is to forget details once you take your eyes and mind away from a task for a few days. Use an app (I like Evernote) to store images and add notes to clarify them. If you're more old school, make a sketch and label the parts to go with your notes and store them all in a folder.

11. But I Just Want to Get Cracking

Actually, patience is still a virtue (especially with springs) and sometimes stuff will fight you, so take your time. If something bursts open because you pulled too hard, it may be impossible for you to see how the internal components fitted together. This is especially true for anything that contains springs or sprung loaded stuff like locks. Be extremely careful with springs at all costs... trust me on this!

12. Electricity is Still Dangerous Stuff

Learn how to isolate the main power in your house in case of emergency. Open up that scary cupboard under the stairs (or wherever yours is) and learn what each circuit does in your fuse box.

Then you'll be able to flip the switch (breaker) and isolate any area of the house in an emergency or before working on a wire.

However, one caveat: Never trust the fuse or circuit breaker description written inside the box. It's a guide. There is no way of knowing if anyone has altered the circuit since the description was written (always test first).

If you need to use power tools, run an extension lead from the non-isolated part of the house (or a neighbours) plugged into a safety breaker such as an RCD (Residual Current Device). RCD's protect you from electrical shock by switching off your device in a few milliseconds if it detects a problem.

Always clearly tape any closed breakers to warn others not to switch them back on.

Remember again, the golden, never to be broken rule 'isolate first and test' before touching anything with fingers.

13. What do I do if I Get a Leak?

You don't need me to tell you that it needs to stop ASAP. But do you know how? Don't wait until you have a problem. Be prepared by going and finding out how to switch off (isolate) the whole water supply to your house right now, go on, this is important, I'll not write another word till you do...

p.s. (most likely it will be somewhere stupid like under the kitchen sink, buried under a load of stuff, or in some random cupboard somewhere...)

... good, you found it? That's called a stopcock, turn it clockwise and the water will stop. Now you know what it looks like and what it does. You'll thank me for this if you're ever unlucky enough to hammer a nail through a stupidly positioned pipe (plumbers eh!?).

It's also a good idea to keep a few emergency repair supplies in the house if there's even a remote possibility you could damage your water pipes or own anything which could potentially leak.

Ask Google "emergency pipe repairs" or better still just go to the local plumbers' merchant and ask for the same.

Emergency repairs range from a roll of special (very!) sticky tape you wind around the pipe to seal the hole, right up to a clever gadget you simply clamp onto the pipe over the hole and fasten the clip.

Some of these emergency repairs can be left as permanent, others need fixing properly at some point in the non-too-distant future.

14. Shoot! My Stopcock is Stuck Solid

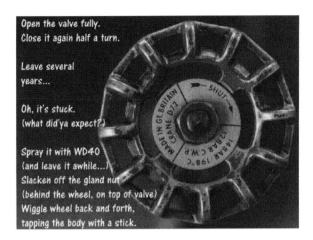

Open the valve fully.
Close it again half a turn.

Leave several
years...

Oh, it's stuck.
(what did'ya expect?)

Spray it with WD40
(and leave it awhile...)
Slacken off the gland nut
(behind the wheel, on top of valve)
Wiggle wheel back and forth,
tapping the body with a stick.

Stopcocks are often found in really stupid locations and because they live in the dark and rarely used, they are often far from easy to close when you really need them.

Stop cocks or water valves stick because folks open them fully and then leave them there. Over time, a valve stuck hard in the fully open stop is very difficult to persuade to move again.

The correct way is to open them fully and then close them half a turn or so. This enables a little 'wiggle' room for the valve next time you need to move it.

If I know I'm going to open an old valve, I'll use a penetrating lube the day before on the valve, (WD40 or such like).

If your stopcock is properly stuck, use a lubricant first and leave it awhile, then try tapping gently around the valve with a timber stick (never anything metal...) at the same time as trying to 'rock' the valve back and forth (oh, and don't forget to pray...).

Some valve designs have a gland nut (behind the wheel where the stem goes into the valve), which you can loosen slightly to relieve pressure on the seal/washer etc. (prepare for some small weeping/leaking when the valve finally moves). Use extra leverage like wrenches on the valve at your peril, you might get away with it or it could go horribly wrong...

From now on, close and re-open yours once a year as a preventative measure.

15. Shush! Listen. What's That Noise?

Everything makes some noise, however small, so keep your ears open (is that even possible?) and really listen to stuff! Listen out for the 'normal' sounds your stuff makes when things are working okay. Knowing exactly how stuff should sound will make you more aware of new or unusual sounds.

Treat any new sound as a warning, because inevitably it does mean there's a problem. Remember each bump, creak, squeeeek, groan, tap, knock, squeal, and rattle means something. It means something's changed and although change might be good for us, it's terrible for most machines or physical things because it usually indicates a problem such as wear or even an impending failure.

As the surfaces of moving parts gradually wear, the tolerance or the space between the parts increases, which leads to more movement, and more movement means more noise. This extra movement is usually microscopic and so the increase in noise might be small and constant, a low-level drone or wine, or even just a different pitch to normal for example.

Some wear related noise might only be apparent when under a particular load. i.e. the noise is worse when under a light or a heavy load. Heavy loads can tighten up some things and quieten them and conversely some things become noisier when under a heavy load (go figure!).

Intermittent sounds might indicate something is moving around unexpectedly. If something has broken rather than worn for example, if parts are in alignment one minute, but not the next, or if something works in one position okay, but not in another.

But most sounds are uniform, timber should sound solid if tapped (not dull) and a motor should run free and constant with no stutters. Heavy things sound dense, hollow things ring and good things sound different to rotten things etc.

A good brick or tile will 'ring' like a bell when tapped, but a cracked one will sound dull.

Motors or mechanical movements like levers, cogs, pulleys, drivebelts, wheels etc. often sound rhythmic, melodic even, when they're working fine. It's a bit like the clickety clack of a train, you soon start to notice when something is disharmonious... if you're listening for it and recognise something has changed. Even Harley Davidson motorcycle engines, which produce a cacophony of crackles, clatters, and pops when you first hear them, have a uniformity and rhythm to their sound if you actually listen to them.

16. A Stethoscope? But I'm Not a Doctor

Because they are great fun! Trust me, I'm a builder, (and I know that's not as good as 'trust me I'm a doctor' but I'm working with what I've got okay?). And I really do have a stethoscope...

You can often diagnose failing components as they break up internally using a simple stethoscope. I use one (very cheaply available from an auto parts store) to identify failing bearings or difficult to trace noises on machines.

The sounds a stethoscope reveals are miraculous in their ability to show whether moving parts are happy or not. You don't even need any special tools to take advantage of this, mechanics used to touch a long wooden stick onto a suspected bad part, pop their thumb over the top, and then press their ear to their thumb. You can make an even better one with a length of narrow metal pipe with a short length of tubing pushed over it. Touch the metal tube to the suspect part and put the tube up to your ear.

Just be careful if there any moving parts, you don't want to get pulled into an engine by your ears!

17. Blah, Blah, Blah, or Not?

Tune in when you hear people talk about their DIY projects. Listen out for any problems, to learn what happened and what they did to fix it. Listening to other people's stories will also help you identify who is knowledgeable about DIY in your circles, these are the guys to ask for help in the future if you get stuck on your own project.

18. Touchy, Feely Stuff is Good for DIY

Touchy, feely stuff really works, and not just on your partner! BUT FIRST, think about what you're going to touch, is it safe? I know it's mostly obvious, but I'll say it anyway, be especially careful around...

- Electricity, even static or low volts (isolate or ground yourself).
- Hot things, elements, bulbs etc. (wait until cool).
- Things that move or could potentially move (secure first).
- Anything sharp and not just actual cutting blades etc.
- Chemicals, including dry powders like cement, plaster etc.
- Heavy or awkward objects or materials (support well).
- Unstable, loose, or unsecured stuff.
- Always tuck in and secure lose hair/clothing.
- Angry or annoyed partners, because you didn't fix that thing...

Start to take notice of and familiarise yourself with how things feel on a day to day basis. Reach out and touch things, hold them, get a sense of how they feel in operation. Mechanical components have a distinctive feel to them when they're running smoothly.

Your sense of touch when handling materials can also tell you a lot about them; if a length of timber feels unusually heavy it may have high moisture content and could shrink excessively. If cement feels lumpy inside the bag, it's soaked up moisture from somewhere and is now pretty useless.

Notice what feels normal with your stuff before there's a problem. Develop a 'sixth sense' for when things are 'off' and file this touchy-feely stuff away to use as a reference for that moment when it 'feels different somehow'.

19. What Does Vibration Tell Me?

Good vibrations are not just for the beach boys, often the first inkling that something is about to fail, or break is a slight difference in the 'feel' or vibration. You might even notice a 'missing' feeling (as in misfiring or rapid on/off), or even a definite and distinct roughness in the running.

Most moving things should feel consistent and smooth. You can feel the vibrations of the gearbox in a car through the gear lever, for example. You can even feel the contact a vehicle has with the road through the tyres, if you really concentrate!

20. Can I learn Anything When It's Off?

Try turning rotary things when they're switched off to see how they feel. Because when things start to break up internally, you might feel a grinding or roughness as you turn them by hand. This usually means failing bearings for example. A hit and miss or on/off feel might mean a problem with missing or worn gears (causing them to slip or not mesh together properly).

21. Can I Feel Something Too Small to see?

Yes. Sometimes you'll be able to feel the tiniest of movements, even ones not, or hardly visible to the naked eye. For example, if you have a car, try jacking up a front wheel (use an axle stand under the chassis). Then grasp the wheel and try to move it from side to side (3 and 9 o'clock) and you might feel the steering mechanism move a little. Now try moving the wheel from top to bottom (12 and 6 o'clock); on modern vehicles, you shouldn't feel anything. Try spinning the wheel round and round, what do you feel?

As before, stuff should be smooth, if you can feel anything or any roughness, something is catching or worn.

22. How Hot is Too Hot?

Most things get warm when running or in use but try to compare with how hot you'd expect it to be in normal use. Faulty electrical parts often increase current load, causing overheating of wires or components.

Many things get warm in use and some too hot to touch, (heaters, engines, exhaust pipes etc).

But if something is hotter than normal, shows scorch marks or is blackened, then something is wrong (like the cracked and dry joints on this PCB for example).

Also, check for proper lubrication, because something running tight creates extra friction which produces heat. Worn bearings also get hot (compare one side to another if applicable).

23. Seriously, You Want me to Thump it?

Almost. Thumping the top of old TV sets was a classic 'fix' when there was a problem. Strangely enough they might have been onto something. Try moving, shaking, twisting stuff etc. Very often stuff with broken wires will start working again, if only intermittently, but it might just be enough to give you a clue about what has happened.

Recently for example, our washing machine's display would flicker and click alarmingly, a sharp tap on the top of the machine just above the display stopped it immediately. Further investigation found a dry connection on the PCB, easily fixed with a soldering iron and a blob of solder...

24. Always Protect Your stuff

Be gentle. Be merciless in using dustsheets or thin sheet material (thick cardboard or even hardboard etc.) to protect things, every time. Use soft jaws in a vice to hold delicate items, use soft hammers made from hide, copper, plastic or even wood to gently tap stuff in to place.

Never dump stuff onto hard surfaces, always put something down first. Put cardboard or old carpet underneath your tools whilst you're working etc.

25. I Need to Smell it? (Ugh!)

Learn how things smell. Especially in conjunction with your other senses i.e. use smells to reinforce a diagnosis. E.g. you might see a leak first, but your sense of smell might help to identify the liquid. Alternatively, you might not be able to see anything, but your sense of smell tells you there's a problem somewhere.

Ozone smells can mean badly running electric motors, damaged contacts, worn out brushes or armatures etc., often described as the 'electric train smell'. And obviously smoke is never good, unless your camping...

26. Keep Brochures and Instructions

Seriously. Always, always, always keep the brochures, guarantees and instructions that come with the stuff you buy. Especially keep any parts list or diagrams and exploded

images as these become invaluable if you need to inside to make repairs.

Keep them in a file or a ring binder with plastic inserts or pockets which are ideal for the little booklets many things come with.

27. Why are Keywords so Important?

They are crucial. Forgive me if you already know all this, but for those that don't.... the words you use to search for something on the internet are called keywords, and search engines understand nothing else.

You need to be very specific with your choice of words or you'll get irrelevant results, millions of them probably. Here are some keywords you could try adding to your query or search, depending what you're looking for...

- The manufacturers name, Bosch, Siemens, Volvo, Kitchen Aid etc.

- The specific model name, type, or number.

- Actual serial numbers taken from the label or box.

- Use words to identify parts affected, e.g. switch, handle, motor, etc.

- Use words that describe your problem, e.g. not working, stopped, makes noise, does a specific thing etc.

- Try informal names for your item or slang words.

- Try different regional words, e.g. tire vs. tyre or silencer vs. muffler or fixing vs. fastener etc.

- Try trade or brand names which have become generic terms or even verbs. Formica, Hoover, Jet Ski, Q-tips, Scotch tape, Sellotape, Sharpie, Tupperware, Velcro etc. etc. are all brand names which are now a part of common language.

- Try alternative words which have similar meanings: fix or mend or repair or adjust or overhaul or rectify, and so on.

- Try words like 'exploded parts diagram' or 'parts list'.

- Try adding 'tutorial' to your keywords.

- Start your search with 'How to fix [insert item here]'

- Try adding 'owners club' or 'fan club',

- Try adding 'blog' or 'forum'.

- Try adding 'customer service' or 'help' or 'online support' or 'advice line' or 'reviews' or 'technical help' etc.

- Last but definitely not least, look for the word 'FAQ'; and nope, it's not cockney wordplay for "what the faq's gone wrong?" it means 'frequently asked questions' and they are frequently asked for a reason... (i.e. it's a common failure point etc.).

You can combine any of the above. Search engines add importance to the words at the beginning of your search query, so put the most relevant stuff first.

"Getting information off the Internet is like taking a drink from a fire hydrant"

Mitchell Kapor

Try to think what someone else would write when looking for whatever it is you need. Try phrasing your query as a question someone is likely to ask, 'how to fix a leaky tap' or even 'my faucet is leaking' for example.

28. Pictures Will Save You Time

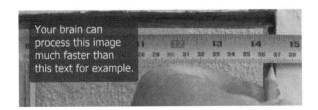

Your brain can process this image much faster than this text for example.

Because images are easier for your brain. One of the quickest ways to find great results on the web is to hit the images tab on your search engine, limiting the results to just images.

Because your brain can take in huge amounts of information visually, it's much faster than reading the normal text results for example.

29. Watch Serious DIY Videos

Video is king. And that's because it's the perfect medium for instructional tutorials. Use the same keyword rules we looked at above to find useful videos, (and don't get distracted by cute cats or dancing parrots...).

30. Aren't Online Forums 'Old Fashioned'?

Folks still flock to online forums to rant about stuff that's gone horribly wrong. And thus, are still one of the best ways to find the answer to your problem. They're usually populated by real enthusiasts, but be aware they don't tolerate fools gladly, so be nice and don't forget to give as well as take (i.e. always report back with updates or the outcomes of your problem, which might help others in the future).

31. Don't Forget Technical Departments

If you have a problem with something, don't be afraid to contact manufacturers. All the good ones have technical departments where you can get free help and advice (some are better than others, but it's a good first stop, and free).

If you can't find a technical department number on your literature or online, try calling any numbers you do find, (sales usually) and ask the person to transfer you to a technical representative or give you their direct number.

32. Are Books Still Relevant?

Hey, you're reading this one! They are becoming a little 'old skool' of course, but they are still very useful as only rarely does someone write a book who doesn't have a passion and good understanding of the topic.

Especially if you can match the age of the publication to the age of the item/problem in question. For example, I have a set of books from the turn of the century which are invaluable to me, because some of the houses I work on were built... yup, you guessed it, around the turn of the century. Bang up to date info if you look at it the right way!

Once there was a time before the internet and do you know, it ticked along pretty well, so don't dismiss the offline world when it comes to finding information.

The cheapest way is to try your local library and don't forget to ask if they have access to a bigger database of books, because many have inter-library lending schemes, hugely increasing the number of books available to you.

Ask library staff if there's any information available that's not physically in the library. It's estimated that the deep web is 500 times larger than the 'surface web' so Note: Part of the deep web includes the dark web, which is the parts of the internet deliberately hidden from the outside world, mostly for legal reasons, but still, you don't want to go wandering around in there, nope, best not, because there are all sorts of funny folks in there...

33. What About Magazines?

Magazines cover every topic imaginable, and they have one great advantage, the information is pretty current. Plus, they have great archives.

Look out for special 'teaser' subscriptions where you can sign up for just one or three copies for very little money. This usually gives you access to any online archives they have as well. Sign up and then download as much as you can before the subscription runs out! Don't forget to cancel it at the end of the cheap period though.

34. Watching TV Can be Work? Awesome!

TV can provide interesting inspiration for your own projects. Keep a notebook (or your phone) handy to record anything that interests you. Listen out for advice from seasoned handy people on TV, I know some home makeover shows can be irritating, but you'll probably learn useful nuggets that might help you one day.

Check your TV listings for home improvement, home makeover or self build re-runs and copy the tips and techniques they use on your own projects.

35. Is it Rude to Ask People You Know?

I know you don't like to bother anyone because you might think your questions are 'stupid', but here's the thing. People LOVE talking about their projects, what they did and how much money they spent or saved. So don't be shy, ask away (at an appropriate time of course).

"From the errors of others, a wise man corrects his own."
Publilius Syrus

36. Old Folks Forget Stuff Don't They?

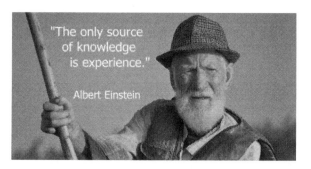
"The only source of knowledge is experience."
Albert Einstein

Hey, I'm 'nearly' old! Don't be too quick to dismiss 'old' people. And no, I don't mean someone over thirty, I mean someone who is a genuine senior. Because regardless of what people under twenty think, older people are a goldmine of knowledge and often have useful skills or experience to share.

I know my Dad tries to tell me how to do stuff all the time (even if I'm not asking...).

37. How Can I Learn More About My home?

Get intimate with your home. Examine all the nooks and crannies, and yes, especially the scary places like under the floorboards, that dark cupboard under the stairs and especially in the attic.

Start with these simple things...

- Check which way the floor boards go because this tells you which way your floor joists run, (joists run perpendicular or 90° to the floor boards).

- Find which walls have floor joists going into them (usually the joists go into the walls parallel to the floor boards, as noted above) this means the wall is load bearing.

- Follow the wires from your fuse box and find out where the main routes are around the house. Look for runs (removed or disturbed floorboards etc.) or access panels and ducts if you're lucky.

- Follow any water and any heating pipes you can see and learn how to isolate them. Again, look for runs and feel for warm floorboards (probably a pipe under there). Access panels might reveal shut off valves etc.

- Examine your walls to find out what materials they used and how thick they are etc. (measure them at doorways or windows).

- Look in any basements, crawl spaces or attics; what can you see? Pipes, wires, tops of walls, timberworks etc.

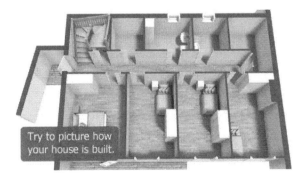

Try to picture how your house is built.

Try to picture your home as an empty shell, ignore all the finished stuff. Picture the walls, the floors, the ceilings, and roof, how does it all sit together? Does everything make sense? What sits on top of what?

If you find parts that don't look logical, you might have hidden structural things like steel beams supporting stuff.

Try to get copies of the original builder's drawings (try the local planning and building control dept.).

38. Incompetents, Idiots, and Iguanas, Eh?

None of the above produce good work. So be aware that not everyone is as good as they should be, i.e. there are some very poor tradesmen and unscrupulous homeowners abound. Don't assume that everything in your house is exactly as it should be. You could find all sorts of anomalies depending on how good the previous guys were.

39. But I Don't Have Any Experience

You have way more than you think. Plus, your own experience and observations will give you 100% reliable information, because no one knows your stuff as well as you do. I guess we've all taken a car to a mechanic only for it to behave faultlessly...

It's often quoted that Michelangelo was 87 years old when he uttered the words "I am still learning" ... He probably didn't say that according to the academics, but semantics aside, be like Michelangelo! Always be learning and adding to your experience to solve future problems.

40. Listen Out for the Warning Bells

Never ignore warning bells. Things do not have bad days or moods or personalities (arguably, some old stuff does, but that's another book). If something looks, sounds, or feels different, then something has changed.

They signal that something 'not nice' is going to happen. It could mean something extra's in the works (a foreign body like grit or water), or you're losing something (metal wearing away or something is leaking).

As we talked about earlier, train your sub-conscious to notice and register tiny details as you go about your routine and put them on your mental radar. Your sub-conscious is powerful and largely idle, so tell it to monitor the clickity clack for that one time when it goes clackity click; because it might just save the day.

41. Intuition is Usually Right (so don't ignore it!)

"Experience is the one thing you can't get for nothing."

Oscar Wilde

Very closely related to the above I know, but in addition to watching out for the actual physical changes around you, also listen to the little voice inside you.

Intuition or insight is the little flash of 'knowing' that might just stop you from making a mistake. It doesn't even come as a fully-fledged thought, but rather as a little niggle in the back of your mind.

It's easy for the uninitiated to ignore, but learn to recognise it, to trust it and to act. First, stop what you're doing and think for a moment; give it time to come to you.

If nothing comes, mentally go through what you're doing again to encourage the niggle to turn into something concrete you can act on. Learn to listen to your intuition and you'll have a powerful ally in your camp to avoid screw-ups, big and small.

42. Practice Makes Perfect (corny but oh, so true)

And yes, I know you don't want to hear this part but... as Clarence Day once said; 'information's pretty thin stuff unless mixed with experience,' and the best way to gain experience is to practice.

"Practice yourself in little things, and thence proceed to greater"

Epictetus

And yet, most folks seem bemused by the concept of practicing DIY skills (can you think of anything else you'd do without practicing?)

Play around with scrap materials, practicing sawing straight (over and over again), by cutting a length of timber up like a bread loaf, hammer in a bunch of nails or drive in a load of screws...

43. Practice by Helping Others

"Of all parts of wisdom, the practice is the best."

John Tillotson

Not many people would turn down the offer of an extra pair of hands on a project. Even if all you can do is pass tools, carry material, or help to clear up, you'll get to learn what each tool is and what it does and how important a clean and tidy workplace is.

You'll also learn about different materials, going to the store, loading and storing them safely. You'll learn about the process and order of work. You could also volunteer to make the vast quantities of coffee all properly planned projects need...

Most importantly, when helping, treat nothing as irrelevant or boring... ever; because there's always something to learn. Even the most mundane task will teach you something about procedure or technique, but only if you're receptive enough to notice it.

44. Sweeping up is Important (More Than You Think)

For example, sweeping up should teach you that...

- A clean and tidy workplace is a safe workplace (you'll have no accidents because you're not falling over stuff).

- A tidy workplace is more productive (because you know where everything is and access to tools and materials is good).

- A clean workplace gives you a more pleasant working experience.

- A clean workplace keeps your clothes cleaner and stops dust and muck spreading throughout the rest of your place.

- A tidy site makes other people 'on site' happy (read the other half/client/neighbours/children etc.).

45. There Are No Stupid Questions

Woodrow Wilson commented that he not only used all the brains that he had, but all that he could borrow.

Ask questions if you don't understand, "it's better to ask a 'stupid' question than to make a stupid mistake"'... so ask away!

Regardless of how handy you are, you'll learn from those around you. I've worked with hundreds of people over the years and I've learned something from all of them, (sometimes something small and occasionally something revelatory). Take advantage of the fact that everyone's knowledge or experience is unique and learn from them.

46. Warning: Do Try This at Home

Just like learning to ride a bicycle, there comes a point where you need to stop thinking about it and make a start.

"I am always doing that which I cannot do, in order that I may learn how to do it."
Pablo Picasso

Learning from mistakes and experimentation is an important part of learning most things, and DIY is no different.

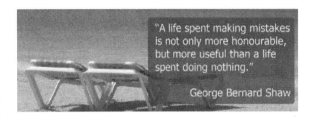
"A life spent making mistakes is not only more honourable, but more useful than a life spent doing nothing."
George Bernard Shaw

47. Nothing is a Total Waste of Time

Nothing is a waste of time if you use the experience wisely. Every little project will teach you a little more about what works or doesn't work with each tool and material.

Plus, you'll learn where your weaknesses are and what tool or material needs more practice.

"Anyone who's never made a mistake has never tried anything new."
Albert Einstein

48. Always Strip before Bin (no not you, the thing!)

Before chucking stuff away, open it up. Take apart something that's going into the recycle bin (i.e. where it doesn't matter if you break something). Open it up and have a look inside. Try to identify the different components; where does the power come in for example or try to figure out what each part does.

49. Always Make Yourself Comfortable

Lastly here, make yourself comfortable (nope, not on the sofa...) I mean don't struggle. Make the time to look after yourself, take breaks eat well, have a hot drink (or a cold one) when you need one i.e. be comfortable.

50. Keep Warm, you'll be Happier (and safer)

Wear proper working clothes. It used to be a kind of culture on UK building sites to wear scrappy clothes and we'd always be cold. Don't do it, buy some warm gear. Charity shops work well for this.

Plus, being cold is dangerous, if you can't feel your fingers and toes, you'll be clumsy and could hurt them and hardly notice. Being numb from cold also leads to poor quality workmanship.

51. Keep Cool Baby

If it's scorching hot, start real early in the morning, at first light if you can manage it (like 4 or 5am!). Then take the afternoons off and go do something fun to cool down. There's nothing better than an early start in the summertime now is there?

52. Understanding How Tools Work

Understanding the basic operation of a tool is fundamental in mastering it.

Always remember... let the tool do the work!

Pick up the tool and look at the different parts. Try to identify what part actually does the work and where does your hand naturally sit? What does it say in the instructions about the best way to hold it properly?

Most tools need multiple inputs to operate correctly; for example, you need to align it properly, to apply a suitable force and use it at a suitable speed. For example, most handsaws have teeth that cut on the front edge, so put the effort into the push stroke to cut the timber and don't waste energy putting pressure on the return or pull stroke because there's no

cutting action there (unless it's a Japanese pull saw).

If it's a new tool, go and watch a video of someone using one on YouTube first to get an idea of what to expect.

53. Perfect Alignment Matters

Tools such as screwdrivers and drill bits need to be perfectly in line with the job. Saws, spanners, and wrenches etc. need to be 90° to the work surface or fastener. Hammers are a bit of both, the head is in line and the handle is at 90° to the job in hand. Wood chisels can be at 90° to chop deep or held at 0° to shave something flush.

54. May the Force be With You

No young Jedi, not that kind of force, I mean the force that does the work. Usually by transferring the power of your muscles or a motor into motion of some kind.

Sticking with screwdrivers as an example; if you put a screwdriver into a screw head and simply turned it, the screwdriver pops straight back out again, likely damaging the relatively soft screw head. It's only when you apply a downward force and at the right angle to prevent the screwdriver from lifting out, as well as a turning force, that the screw turns instead of lifting out.

55. Judgement (don't panic, it's not the holy kind)

Practice until you can judge just how much force is enough for each tool and the task in hand. Too little and it won't do the work, too much and the tool can slip as the force exceeds the grip of the tool, again especially important with cordless power screwdrivers (learn to judge what setting the safety clutch needs to be on, till it slips just right).

56. Listen. No, No, I Mean Really Listen

One trick with power tools is to hold firmly and push steadily and listen to the motor/ blade. It should only slow down a little: Don't 'bog down' the blade (i.e. nearly stop it!).

Listen to motors. Don't push too hard, most tools should only slow down a little (guestimate around 10%) for best results. Let the tool do the work!

57. Blunt Tools are Mistake Makers

Learn the relationship between bad/blunt tools and force/effort. For example, worn, blunt or chipped screwdrivers, chisels, saws, files, or snips need much more force to do the same work than their sharp or well-fitting counterparts.

This excessive force in conjunction with the blunt edges and poor gripping surfaces increases the likelihood of the tool slipping.

When a tool slips, remember all that excessive force must go somewhere, (usually uncontrollably) and you'll likely damage the workpiece or yourself.

58. When More is Better

Sometimes you need more power. A wrecking or crow bar is a great example. These massively multiply the pressure you can bring to bear on an object by using a long lever over a fulcrum to move a short lever.

The turning force of a wrench is easily multiplied by slipping a length of tube or pipe over the handle, lengthening it and thus the force it applies.

59. Nee Nah, Nee Nah: You're Nicked!

Lever the spanners against each other and break the lock

Lost your key?

A 'naughty' example: choose a pair of spanners which just fit into the hasp (U shaped bit) of a padlock and with the spanner heads together, push the other end of the spanners together like a pair of scissors.

The force is easily enough to break the lock open. Closely followed by the sound of sirens if it's not your padlock, you have been warned...

60. Shock and Awe Works

Levers apply force slowly. But a heavy and sharp application of force can shock things loose (or break them). Hammer around a nut or bolt head with a small hammer can help break the hold of a tight fastener (especially if it's corroded).

But, never hit any exposed threads (not even once!), especially on the end of the bolt, or you'll damage them.

Another example; a hammer and a cold or masonry chisel uses shock to break up bricks or concrete. A powerful hammer blow transmits an exponentially magnified force through the chisel to a tiny area on the very tip of the chisel.

61. Jeeeze, That's Hot!

Another type of force to break super tight stuff apart is to use physics (i.e. heat), on metal things at least (don't try this on anything else!) Gently heat up the offending part with a small heat source, like a plumber's blowtorch or in a pinch, that 'Crème Brulee' blowtorch you got for Christmas (watch out for nearby flammable stuff...).

Concentrate the heat onto the offending part (usually a nut) until it starts to glow. Removing the heat, quickly try again to undo the nut using a wrench and of course thick gloves, (heat travels up wrenches too remember!). The heat forces the nut to expand at a different rate to the bolt, breaking the tightness... hopefully.

62. Jeeeze Louise, That's Cold!

Sticking stuff in the freezer can also help break stuck things. Incidentally, cold, heat, and pressure are forces of nature often used to fasten parts together (called an interference fit). Put the smaller part in the freezer and heat up the larger part and they will slide together easily and yet bond tightly at room temperature.

63. It Can Take the Pressure

A press or friction fit. Huge amounts of pressure will force two parts together. It's common to use a big and powerful hydraulic (or manual screw) press to push a bearing onto a shaft for example.

At home you can improvise with a big vices or long bolts and big washers/ spacers/ sockets etc. to do the same job.

64. Speed, Glorious Speed

Ah, the need for speed! Everybody wants to get the job done as quickly as possible (again blooming 'makeover' TV!). Many tools also have an optimum speed.

Excessive speed, often along with excessive force wastes effort and can go badly wrong because you'll lose accuracy and/or grip. This nearly always leads to damage to you or your workpiece (so slow down!).

65. Mechanical Sympathy

Noticing how your tools sound and feel at speed will help develop your mechanical sympathy, a kind of sixth sense for recognising when a machine is struggling to cope because it's overloaded.

Some folks think the harder they push a tool, the more work they'll do. Overloading tools usually produces less work, because it quickly blunts sharp edges and can really shorten the lifespan of motors etc.

66. High Pressure = Low Speed

Usually, tools or tasks which need high pressure, need a slower speed, undoing a screw for example, or drilling a hole in metal.

67. High Speed = Low Pressure

Faster speeds usually need less pressure as the speed is doing the work, drilling into wood or masonry for example.

"There is time for everything."
Thomas A. Edison

68. Stand Comfortably and Relax

So you've got a new tool and you're ready to give it a try...

- Make sure that you can see the business end of the tool and what it's doing. Use extra lighting if necessary.

- Prepare for the point at which something changes, a plane at the end of a run for example, or a drill bit approaching the back of the material and the classic, a saw blade just about to go all the way through.

- Practice using the tool carefully and deliberately, ensuring the two points above are uppermost in your mind, (support stuff properly!).

- Take your time, rushing about nearly always spoils something or other, either the tool, the material or you...

69. I Screwed Up, Royally

- Did you read the tools operating instructions (duh)?

- Was the tool sharp and/or in good condition?

- Was the tool properly adjusted for the task?

- Were you physically holding the tool properly?

- Did you hold the tool in the proper place, i.e. using the moulded grips if it has them?

- Was the tool aligned correctly with the workpiece?

- Did you look at it from different angles to check?

- Were you pressing too hard or not hard enough?

- Were you positioned comfortably and not over reaching?

- Could you clearly see what you were doing or working on?

- Were you being careful or rushing a little?

- Where did the tool go when it slipped or moved?

- What did the tool do at the point it let go?

- What were you doing at the point when the tool let go?

70. Where's my Blooming Pencil

Practice storing your pencil behind your ear until you can bend down without it falling off... No? Okay, try sharpening it with a razor-sharp wood chisel then, still no? well, I'm afraid there is no hope for you then...

Only joking. Just sharpen it with your Minnie Mouse pencil sharpener and keep it in your side pocket, I'm not judging...

Always, sharpen your pencil. I know you just did it but do it again for good practice; and anyway, I want to see that Minnie Mouse sharpener again! Plus, a blunt pencil will ruin your accuracy.

When measuring, place a pencil mark exactly on the measurement you need. This makes the exact size in the middle of the pencil mark.

Indicate on the workpiece which side is 'scrap', using a cross, wiggly line, a smiley face or whatever you like.

Cut on the waste side of your pencil mark, aiming to have half the pencil mark still showing on your work piece.

Measure the workpiece afterwards and adjust your 'marking style' next time to increase your accuracy in future. Some folks like

to mark on the outside of their length and then cut all the pencil mark out.

71. Look, My Fingers Are a Marking Gauge

Another marking tip you can do with a pencil is to use it like a marking gauge, creating parallel lines. See next image...

Pinch your fingers together to hold them tight and slide down the workpiece with your pencil

Mind out for splinters!

72. Marking Hole Positions

Be accurate when marking hole positions. Sometimes tiny differences in position can be a real problem, especially on things with no built-in adjustment, (such as simple shelf brackets).

Hold stuff in position and mark through the holes if you can. Be sure to mark the full circle so you'll know where the centre of the hole is. You might need to use a deep hole marker or shave a pencil down for brackets made from thicker material.

73. Shoot, I Found my Knife (and not in a good way)

Don't forget you're all soft, squidgy, full of precious liquid and are very, very easy to damage. Whereas most hand tools are sharp, heavy (or both) and made from hard, unforgiving materials. Always cover the cutting edges of sharp tools in your toolbox to protect them and you.

74. I Can't Find My Whatchamacallit

Don't overcrowd your toolboxes, because it'll frustrate you and waste time as you try to find that particular small tool which always ends up at the bottom.

75. How Long Did I Say It Was?

'Measure twice; cut once' is a folk law for a reason. Double-check your measurements on a notepad with the one in your head before cutting. This is especially useful if you got to cut several pieces, whilst fitting skirting boards around a room for example and the power saw is outside...

76. Easily Measure Inside Stuff

If you want to measure inside something (a cupboard for example), hold the tape blade itself and push the hook end of the tape up to one side and then push the body of the tape measure itself to the other side; press the lock button and read the measurement as it comes out of the casing. Add the width of the tape itself (printed on the side of the case) to get the total.

Also, never hold the hook against the inside of something with your thumb and then pull the tape out and measure, you'll be the thickness of the hook short (see next tip). Always push the tape up to the surface when measuring inside for the best accuracy.

77. It's Supposed to be Loose

The hook on the end of a tape measure 'floats' to allow you to take external (and internal) measurements. The amount of float equals the thickness of the metal hook at the end you see.

78. Shoot, Now I've Cut it Too Short

Get into the habit of pushing the tape along until the hook just drops over the end (rather than shooting the tape past the end of the material, drawing it back) and then pulling it tight.

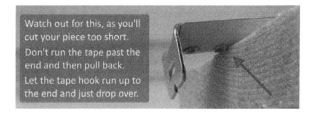

Watch out for this, as you'll cut your piece too short. Don't run the tape past the end and then pull back. Let the tape hook run up to the end and just drop over.

Cheap tapes especially are prone to snag on the rivets holding the hook.

79. The Little Slot is There for a Reason

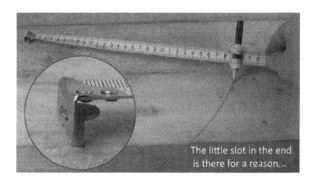

The little slot in the end is there for a reason...

You can draw circles by hooking the little slot in the end of the tape over a convenient nail in the centre of your circle and use an elastic band to hold a pencil at your desired radius, (you always wondered what the slot was for huh?).

80. Use a Tape for Parallel Cuts

Similar to the 'using a pencil as a marking gauge' tip we looked at earlier, you can cut (or just mark) parallel cuts by pinching the blade of the tape at your desired width.

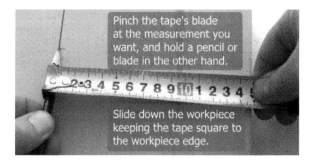

Pinch the tape's blade at the measurement you want, and hold a pencil or blade in the other hand.

Slide down the workpiece keeping the tape square to the workpiece edge.

Then using your fingers as a guide, slide along the workpiece, holding a craft knife (or pencil) at the end of the tape with your other hand. It's a bit fiddly and takes some practice, but once mastered, it's an easy way for plasterers to cut long parallel pieces of drywall.

81. Never Store a Wet Tape

If you get a tape wet, grab a dry rag, pull out the whole tape, and run it all back in slowly through the rag to dry it off. Store it somewhere warm overnight if you can. It'll go rusty in hours if you don't.

82. If you're Working Alone

Get yourself a good quality digital or laser measure, especially if you often work alone. They're especially useful for measuring internal dimensions or long lengths of trims in awkward locations like up near the ceiling for example.

83. You Don't Always Need a Tape Measure

Don't use a tape measure if you don't have to. If appropriate, hold up the workpiece, push it into place one end and mark the cut directly on the other end. Great for small trims etc.

84. How to Measure Small Round Stuff

Best to use a calliper, but if you don't have one, use an adjustable spanner /wrench as a crude calliper to measure the diameter of small round things (bolts, drill bits etc.). Then either measure the distance between the wrench jaws, or just use the jaws to physically compare a drill bit and bolt for example.

85. Hammers: A Hammer is a Hammer

Never use any other tool as a hammer because you'll struggle and might damage the workpiece (not to mention the tool).

86. Hammers: One Time Where Size Matters

It's essential the size of the hammer (thus force) matches the situation, i.e. small stuff = small hammer, bigger stuff needs, yup, you guessed it, a dirty great big hammer. Never use a large hammer lightly or a little hammer aggressively (you'll look funny...).

87. Hammers: Keep it in Line

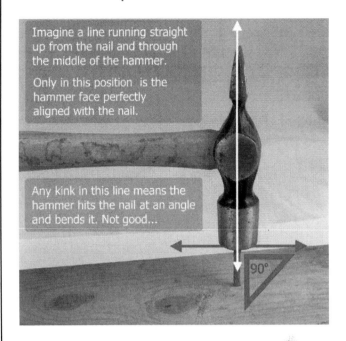

Imagine a line running straight up from the nail and through the middle of the hammer.

Only in this position is the hammer face perfectly aligned with the nail.

Any kink in this line means the hammer hits the nail at an angle and bends it. Not good...

90°

Picture hitting the nail with the head (top part) of the hammer completely in line with the nail, as this ensures the actual face of the hammer is 90° to the nail head, i.e. hitting it squarely.

Practice just touching the nail with your hammer a few times, like a golfer practices his swing before hitting the ball... (you can mutter something profound as you do this if you like...).

88. Hammers: Hold it Steady

Try keeping a hold of the nail (if you dare!) and (relatively gently) tap the nail until it's about a quarter of its length in, then the nail will be sturdy and less likely to bend if you slightly miss-hit it; mind your fingers though...

89. Stop Before You're All the Way In (steady!)

Finish off the last few blows carefully to avoid unsightly 'half-moons' where the hammer hits the wood on the last stroke. Once the nail head is flush, or almost flush with the timbers surface, consider using a nail punch to drive the nail below the surface for best results.

You'll probably need a couple of different sized nail punches. One tiny one for pins and a bigger one for larger nails like lost heads etc.

90. Ouch! If You Keep Hitting Your Fingers

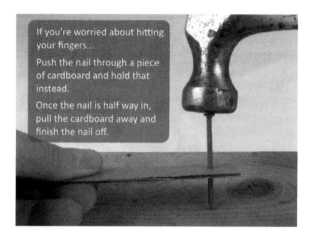

If you're worried about hitting your fingers...

Push the nail through a piece of cardboard and hold that instead.

Once the nail is half way in, pull the cardboard away and finish the nail off.

91. If You Keep Bending the Blooming Nails

It usually means the hammer is hitting the nail at a slight angle. The head must hit the nail head perfectly flat to drive it in straight.

If you very slightly miss hit a nail and it bends slightly one way, make the next blow slightly more towards the side in which the nail is leaning to send it back over the other way to straighten it.

92. Too Late, It's Bent

If you've bent a nail, use your claw hammer to straighten up the worst of it. Like this...

Grab the nail in between the claw and twist the hammer in a rotating, upwards motion.

Concentrate your effort on the nail above the bend, not the bottom part of the nail.

And then use a club hammer on one side and your claw hammer on the opposite side to 'dress' the nail straight again before continuing.

Like so...

Work around and up and down the nail, 'dressing' it straight.

93. I'm Doing it Right But...

If you find the hammer is still skidding off the nail and you're convinced you're hitting it squarely... try the old tradesman's trick and sandpaper the striking face of the hammer to remove the polished surface before trying again.

94. When You're Close to the Edge

Nails are basically small wedges and if you're nailing close to the end of a piece of wood it'll split.

Tap the point on a nail to flatten it. The flat end punches a hole through the timber fibres (instead of just pushing them aside, which creates pressure).

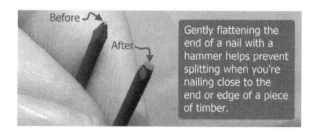

Before

After

Gently flattening the end of a nail with a hammer helps prevent splitting when you're nailing close to the end or edge of a piece of timber.

95. It's Bouncing all Over the Place

If nailing something which is not sturdy, hold something heavy (a heavy hammer or a brick) on the opposite side. This acts as a counter weight and absorbs some of the force of your blows.

96. When the Nail Keeps Going Back In

Sometimes when you lever something out a little, the nail 'pops out', but promptly disappears again when you release the bar.

Try levering it out again and then use a second claw hammer or bar and 'tap' the part of the nail that emerges from the back piece of timber to dent or bend it slightly.

This often stops it disappearing back into the hole when you let go, popping the nail head out the face side in the process, so you can grab the nail head with the claw.

97. Don't Damage the Surface

Think about which way you lever a bar. Try to lever away from the 'face' surface and into the piece you're throwing away if you can, (pull instead of push for example).

Don't lever against the wall when taking off trims like skirting or base boards, cornices etc., because it'll put a dent in the plasterworks, or even make a hole in drywall.

Use offcuts of timber behind the bar, minimum 25mm × 100mm × 300mm (1″×4″×12″) on masonry and much bigger on drywall (to span between two studs).

The timber will spread the point load out and stop the bar digging into the plaster.

98. Flat Wrecking Bars Are Brilliant

Get one of the modern flat, thin pry bars as the fine end makes getting into the smallest of gaps a cinch.

99. Don't Start in the Middle

When levering stuff off or apart, look for any joints, or start at the end as it's easier to lever up a piece. Staring in the middle has you fighting two fixed ends.

100. Two is Often Better Than One

Two prying implements are good when removing long trims etc. leapfrogging over each other as you work your way down the joint or seam. Typical is a pry bar and your claw hammer or two pry bars.

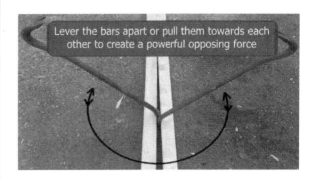

Lever the bars apart or pull them towards each other to create a powerful opposing force

101. Use Old Tools on Rough Work

Save an old wood chisel, screwdriver and wood saw for rough work, I call mine my 'No. 2' tools (because they're crappy!).

Trying to get paint out of an old slotted screw head? Use your No.2 screwdriver. Cutting out an old window frame or ripping out an unwanted door set? Use your No.2 saw so when you catch a nail or some masonry (and you will) it won't matter.

102. Work Safe with Nails

Make it a habit to 'make safe' any protruding nails as you work because handling stuff full of sharp nails is almost impossible to do without hurting yourself. You don't necessarily have to remove the nail from the timber, just knock them through from the backside to make the nail point safe.

103. Reverse Can be Better Than Forward

Pull small nails out from the back using a pair of pincers. Tapping them through from the back with a hammer will splinter the front face.

If you intend reusing trims etc. try pulling the nails through from the backside with a pair of pincers. Pulling small gauge wire or 'air gun' nails out through from the rear is especially easy and leaves the front unmarked.

104. Practice Makes for Easier Sawing

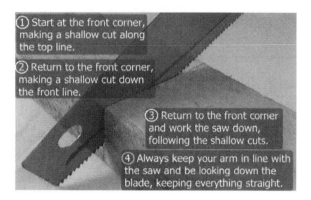

① Start at the front corner, making a shallow cut along the top line.

② Return to the front corner, making a shallow cut down the front line.

③ Return to the front corner and work the saw down, following the shallow cuts.

④ Always keep your arm in line with the saw and be looking down the blade, keeping everything straight.

105. Always have an Exit Strategy

Saw blades need to go into the face side of the workpiece and out of the rear, (this applies to powered saws as well). Note that if you're using a hand-held circular saw, this means cutting from the rear side, (face side down) because the blade rotates up through the workpiece and out of the top.

106. Small Splinters on the Back Edge

If you have some small splintering on the back edge of the workpiece, run a small hand plane or sandpaper at 45° to the cut edges afterwards.

This creates a tiny chamfer which hides small splintering very well (works great on laminated boards like melamine or kitchen worktops etc.).

107. You Paid for the Whole Saw

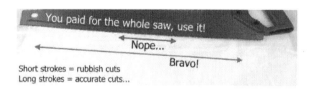

You paid for the whole saw, use it!

Nope...

Bravo!

Short strokes = rubbish cuts
Long strokes = accurate cuts...

You paid for the whole saw, so use all of it; don't just use the middle bit. Seriously, using the whole saw, i.e. long strokes really helps keep the saw in a straight line...

108. Hacksaw Blades

Always have a spare hacksaw blade, because you'll definitely break the blade if you don't have a spare one. If you have a spare blade, the one you have will last forever, it's called Murphy's law.

109. Almost all the Way Through the Metal

On rough metal work (cutting re-bar etc.), you might not need to go all the way through, saw ¾ of the way through or so and then bend the offcut back and forth a couple of times to snap it off, (most metals fatigue quickly to failure point).

110. If it all Goes Horribly Wrong

Remember to wrap any accidentally removed body parts in a clean damp cloth, pop it into a sealable plastic bag, and place the bag in ice cold water or the bottom of the fridge (not freezer) till the ambulance arrives.

Cooling the severed part will keep it viable for half a day or so, but without cooling, that reduces to as little as an hour or two.

NB:

Never put body parts directly on ice as this tends to make stitching them back on much more difficult. Seriously, I'm not joking.

111. Three Secrets to Drilling Holes

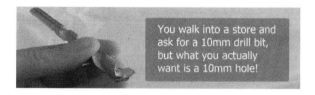

You walk into a store and ask for a 10mm drill bit, but what you actually want is a 10mm hole!

I love the previous image; you can't beat a little philosophy on the job!

- Knowing your material, i.e. what you're drilling into.

- Choosing the right drill bit for that material.

- Using the right technique for that bit in that material.

112. Use the Right Drill Bit

Each material needs a specific bit to drill clean holes safely. If you get this wrong, you'll struggle to make a hole, most likely ruin the drill bit and maybe even hurt yourself if the bit snatches or sticks in the workpiece.

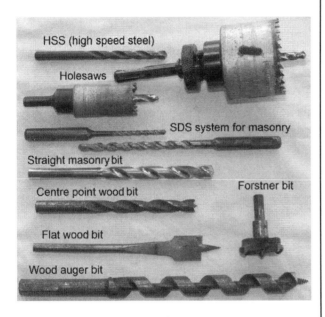

HSS (high speed steel)
Holesaws
SDS system for masonry
Straight masonry bit
Centre point wood bit
Forstner bit
Flat wood bit
Wood auger bit

113. If You Don't want to go Too Deep

A simple way to create a 'depth stop' is to wrap a few turns of electrical tape around the bit at the depth you want to stop at.

Keep a close watch on the tape as you drill, stopping just before the tape hits the surface of the workpiece or you'll push the tape up the bit and drill too deep, potentially ruining your perfectly good day...

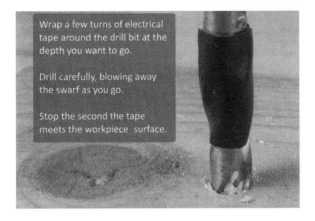

Wrap a few turns of electrical tape around the drill bit at the depth you want to go.

Drill carefully, blowing away the swarf as you go.

Stop the second the tape meets the workpiece surface.

114. Start Slow

Starting very slowly works well in all materials, at least until the drill bit has cut a shallow

depression exactly over your mark. Watch for the drill bit twisting up and away from your mark if you start too fast.

As the hole deepens, you may gradually apply more speed and/or pressure. Listen and get a feel for when the drill bit is clogging up, (it will slow down and sound different). Clear clogged drill bit flutes by backing the bit almost all the way out to allow the swarf (bits of stuff you've drilled out) to clear before plunging back in again. Repeat as often as necessary.

115. Be Alert, Your Country Needs Lerts...

Always be alert for when the drill bit breaks through the other side (when applicable, don't do this when drilling into a party wall...), listen and feel for the bit as it approaches the underside, it'll start to feel and sound different, maybe slowing down a little and a deeper note.

Ease off on the pressure and be ready to pull up the millisecond it goes through, to avoid the drills chuck slamming into your workpiece.

116. People Don't Like Dust on the Floor

Keep things clean; tape an open envelope beneath the hole on a wall or drill through a small plastic pot (aerosol top etc.) if the hole is on the ceiling to catch the dust, or best of all, simply hold a vacuum cleaner nozzle close by as you drill the hole.

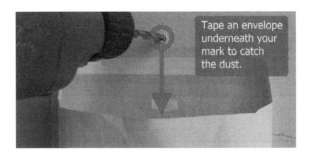

Tape an envelope underneath your mark to catch the dust.

117. Drilling Timber

Many different types of drill bits will cut in wood; even a masonry bit will roughly force its way through a piece of timber when pushed on the hammer setting.

Generally, though, most folks use HSS or twist bits for holes up to 10mm and flat or auger bits between 10 and 25mm or so and then hole saws for large holes from 25mm up to around 100mm or so.

Anything bigger than 100mm or so, it's probably easier to use a jigsaw.

118. Hole Jigs Are Easy, Accurate and Quick

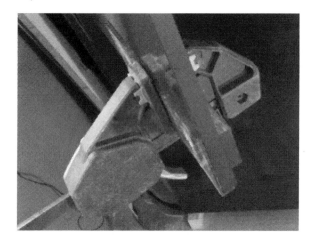

Especially for repeat drilling such as cabinet door handles. Hold them with a quick clamp and pop a piece of scrap wood at the back to get the cleanest holes.

119. Avoid Drilling the Wrong Hole

One wrong hole and you've ruined the job. Always put a piece of tape over the right hole and then drill through the tape in the right place (be 100% sure it's right tho').

This makes it virtually impossible to drill a hole in the wrong place.

120. Quick Clamp Tip for Repeat Clamping

When releasing a quick clamp always twist it a little (up, down or sideways) as you press the release trigger. This will open up the jaws a fraction more, making it much easier to put onto the next position. Ideal for repeat clamping situations like kitchen cabinet handles etc.

121. Self-Centering is a Thing

For super accurate drilling of small mounting holes, such as through a hinge for example, treat yourself to a set of self-centring drill bits. These have a pilot drill inside a spring-loaded chamfered tube. Simply locate the tube into the countersunk hole in the hinge (etc.) and press. The tube self-centres itself and ensures the pilot drill hits the exact centre of the hole. Brilliant!

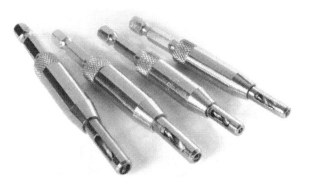

122. Stop Half Way Through

For the cleanest holes use flat or auger bits and drill into the timber until just the tip of the bit shows through on the backside. Then withdraw the bit, turn the workpiece over and carry on from the other side to remove the last part of the hole.

123. Clamp Scrap Wood to the Backside

As with the hole jig, another way of avoiding tear out on the backside is to clamp some scrap timber to the backside and drill through the whole thing.

This way the tear out occurs in the scrap timber and not your finished work piece.

124. If You Drill the Wrong Sized Hole

If you make a mistake with an auger, a spade bit or a hole-saw and drill a 'too small' hole, you're in trouble. Because now there is no centre timber to hold the lead point or guide drill bit.

But don't fear, there is a solution. Grab a piece of scrap wood bigger than the hole you want and drill the right sized hole through it.

Then clamp the hole in the scrap wood over the original 'too small' hole, drill through the scrap wood hole and it will guide the bit into the original hole.

Oh, and if you've drilled a hole that's too big... you're on your own.

125. Drill Bits Exit Like Bullets

Always drill from the 'face' side and never from the backside (inside) or you'll end up with a very large hole in the face side where the drill bit exits.

126. Starting a Hole in Metal

Because metal is hard (duh!), drill bits find it difficult to start and wander or walk all over the place. To avoid this, place a centre punch dead centre of your proposed hole and give it one (and only one) sharp tap with a hammer. The tiny depression gives something for the drill bit to bite into as it starts up.

127. Don't Make a Propeller Blade

Use a vice or clamps to hold metal when drilling holes. Never, ever hold metal in your hands (or feet) when drilling holes. Drill bits snag as they go through the back side every single time, and if the workpiece is not well secured, it turns into a propeller, a very sharp propeller, just picture a lawnmower blade, i.e. it's going to get bloody...

128. Blunt Bits Get Hot and Blunter

Sharp drill bits are essential. You'll need to press a blunt bit harder to get it to cut which causes it to overheat. The more it overheats the blunter it gets and the harder you must press, the harder you press the blunter it gets and... well, you can see where this is going can't you? Use sharp bits!

129. It's Hot, so Use Coolant

Drill bits must not overheat because it alters their hardness and blunts them. Watch the tip for smoke, which means it's getting too hot. Use a coolant for all but the smallest holes in thin material...

Engineers use a special coolant, a thin cutting fluid dripped onto drill bits via a special pump and tube.

You can use WD40 or light oil squirted onto the bit as you drill. In a pinch use water in an old washing up liquid bottle or spray bottle (dry off afterwards to prevent corrosion). Remember: these fluids act as a coolant first and a lubricant second.

130. Is it Sharp?

You can easily see when a drill bit is sharp and you've got the angle right because, as with a wood plane, the shavings (called swarf when drilling) will peel off in long-ish pieces.

If you're getting small chips when drilling steel, then the drill bit is not sharp enough (small chips are normal when drilling brass though because the bits are different).

131. Brass is Special

To drill holes in brass you'll need a bit which has a 90° cutting edge. In effect, the cutting edge scrapes the brass off like a milling machine (in a pinch you can file a small flat on the cutting edge of a regular HSS bit). A regular HSS bit will bite too far into brass and become stuck.

This works to drill plastic too.

132. Big Holes in Metal

Drill a small 'lead hole' first. This makes it much easier for the larger drill bit. For example, if your goal is an 8mm hole, start with a 4mm one first (appx. half the final hole size); then follow with the 8mm bit. For even bigger holes, you can step them in a similar way; 4mm, 8mm, and finally 12mm etc.

133. Stainless Steel is Hard

To drill holes in stainless steel you'll need special bits made from cobalt, titanium, carbide, or diamond etc. plus lots of pressure (feed) in combination with a slow drilling speed and lots of cooling lubricant.

134. Aluminium is a Pussy (comparatively)

Drilling aluminium is easy as it's comparatively soft. But it does clogs drill flutes easily, so try pecking (backing in and out) during drilling to clear the swarf etc.

135. Drilling Tiles, Ceramics, and Glass

Tiles and ceramics have very hard surfaces and some, like porcelain or glass for example are very hard all the way through. You'll need special tile/glass drill bits made from carbide or diamond tips.

Another challenge is getting started (bits tend to wander). Try using masking tape on the tile for small holes.

Personally, I use a non-slip template/guide made from thin plywood with a couple of thin lines of cured silicone sealant on the back. This has a few common hole sizes through it, I simply hold the hole size I need over my perfectly measured and marked holes and use the guide to get the hole started. Once there is a shallow depression, I remove the template and finish the rest of the hole off normally.

Regular masonry drill bits (with tungsten carbide tips) will drill small holes in some ceramic glazed tiles (e.g. 6mm holes for a toilet roll holder etc.).

Don't apply too much feed, tile is the opposite of metal, a medium to high speed and very light feed is usually best for tile.

Remember to switch off the hammer action off and remember you run the risk of overheating the tip and melting the brazing that holds the tungsten carbide tips in place. It's unlikely a masonry bit will drill harder tiles though, porcelain for example.

136. Hole Free Fixings

Small and lightweight stuff easily hangs from special adhesive pads.

Alternatively, hang small and lightweight stuff using silicone sealant...

- Stick the backing plate to the wall with a little silicone and use masking tape to hold it until the silicone sets.

- Then go around the edges with more silicone to reinforce it.

- Leave to cure fully and then assemble the bracket following the instructions.

This works well for lightweight stuff such as toothbrush holders, loo roll holders and such like.

137. Making Holes in Rubber

Use a hollow punch or make one out of a sharpened piece of pipe or similar. Pop the rubber sheet onto a solid block of wood and hold the punch very firmly on your mark. One sharp hit with a hammer works best for the cleanest holes.

138. Drilling Holes in Carpet

Don't do it, trust me, it will go horribly wrong. You'll run the risk of pulling a thread and believe me if the bit 'catches' a thread, it'll run across the whole carpet in a flash, long before you can stop the drill bit... expensive.

Use the same technique as mentioned above for rubber. Some folks like to melt holes using a pipe (or even a socket wrench etc.) heated with a blowtorch (seems a little risky to me though).

139. Simple Template for Back Plates

Remember the 'brass rubbings' you did as a child? You can use that to copy the hole positions of things with multiple holes. For example, keyhole hanging brackets or hinges (see next images).

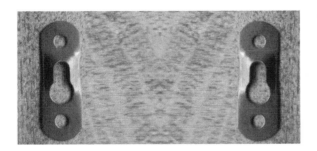

Simply place a sheet of paper over the whole thing, aligned with the top edge and rub a soft pencil over the keyholes etc. and they'll become very clear.

Align the top edge of the paper with your mark for the top on the wall and mark though the paper to get the exact location of the screw or hole positions.

140. It's Never 'Near Enough' (Re: Quality)

Honestly, I just can't stress this enough, it's such a common failing for newbies to think that the job is 'near enough', but it never is. Leaving stuff slightly 'out' of level or plumb etc. will always bite you on the butt later in the project. Either the last part won't fit properly, or you won't be able to adjust a component properly, or a component won't work properly, or it just looks bad.

Make the time to get stuff exactly straight, level, plumb and square because then everything will fit much better with only minimal adjustments needed, saving you lots of time in the end.

141. Start Level = End Level

For example, I've built houses, level from top to bottom hardly using a spirit level to measure horizontals. How? Because I set up the foundations exactly horizontal and measured my brickwork up from that foundation level using my tape measure. If it's level to start with, (and each corner height measures the same), it will still be level at the roof. Oh, how we laughed at teams who threw the concrete into their trenches in a rush and then wasted valuable time trying to get the brickwork level in time to put the windows in.

142. Levels Are Not That Accurate

Turn the spirit level around each time you move to counteract any inaccuracy in the spirit level.

If you're marking out a level line along a wall you must flip the level around, end to end each time you move. This way any inaccuracy within the spirit level itself will even out.

If you keep the spirit level the same way each time you move (and it's 1mm inaccurate), your line could be several mm's out of level by the time you get across the room.

143. Check the Level for Accuracy

You can double-check a spirit level for accuracy by placing it on something horizontal and turning it around through 180° lengthways. The bubble should be in the middle both ways to be truly level. If it shows correct one-way but slightly out when turned around, there may be a problem with the spirit level.

144. It Looks Alright, But...

Optical illusions sometimes make things look bad, so very occasionally it's best to go with what looks right, regardless of what the spirit level bubble is saying.

For example, a bookcase close to a doorway might look better fitted an equal distance from the architrave, creating a parallel gap, even if it's then slightly out of plumb. This is because stuff that tapers can draw the eye and look 'wrong'.

A mate of mine used to work the cruise liners, renovating a certain number of cabins each trip. He said you could always tell the new guys as they still had spirit levels...

145. Home Made Tool to Measure Plumb

If you don't have a good spirit level or you want to check something from floor to ceiling (or higher) use a plumb line (a heavy pointed weight suspended on the end of a thin string or line). You can make your own by tying anything small and heavy to the end of thin string and suspend it where it can hang completely free. Either measure from the line or place marks on the wall behind the string etc. Plumb lines are always 100% accurate, (well, until the planet really starts wobbling that is!)

146. By the Laws of the Universe

(cue dramatic music...), if something is perfectly level and plumb... it must also be square (don't worry about this, it just is okay!).

147. Easy Math. Seriously, It Really Is

You'll remember from school the 'power of Pythagoras' (cue dramatic music again!) The Pythagorean Theorem or 3:4:5 as it's often called on building sites.

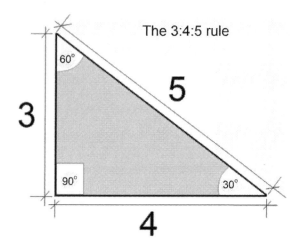

Measure 3 units along one side and 4 along the adjacent side and then measure across the hypotenuse (okay, the long side then). Drum roll please... if it's exactly 5 units, then the corner is square, hallelujah!

It doesn't matter what units you use, if you keep to the ratio, metres, centimetres, inches, feet etc. are all good. Multiples work even better; (6:8:10 or 9:12:15 etc.) because longer lengths increase accuracy.

148. Break Projects into Small Pieces

The trick to avoiding DIY burnout during bigger projects, (or dare I say it, any boring bits), is to break the job into much smaller, more manageable tasks, (both physically and mentally).

Don't focus on the whole project. Focus instead on each small task, each step, each brick, each tile, or each coat of paint etc. At the end of each task look at it, saying 'Wow that looks fantastic; I made a really good job of that.' Then, move on to the next task and repeat.

"Ability is a poor mans wealth"
John Wooden

These small successes add up over time until one day it's finished. Will Smith the actor once said, "don't focus on the whole wall, focus on each brick, the wall will take care of itself". Great advice.

Sure, building something large takes a lot of time, but what 'hobby' doesn't? If you can lay one brick perfectly (even if it takes a minute or two), potentially you can lay a thousand and so on until you've built your house.

Tackle every practical task one piece at a time, one cut, one nail, one screw, one coat of paint etc. Learn each new skill one, easily researched, learnt, and practiced technique at a time.

Breaking stuff down into small, individual tasks is the key to coping with the magnitude of larger jobs and learning the skills you need, one small step at a time.

Even professionals like me need to mentally break down their projects, a joker of a client once pointed to a 20-ton pile of sand and a pile of 20,000 bricks then and said 'right, off you go then, move all that' as he handed me a small trowel...

The only way you get through it, is to look at the work one wall at a time or one day at a time and on bad days, one brick at a time...

In theory, this 'one at a time' method means anyone could do it. If you don't believe me, search online for 'self-build homes' and find thousands of houses, built by amateurs, all over the world, you can even buy kits to get you started.

149. Always be Finishing Something

Each day you plan to tackle a part of your project, it's essential to choose a task that fits the time you have available. For example, if you only have 30 minutes one day, choose to do something that takes 30 minutes to finish. Don't get 30 minutes into a job that's going to take 4 hours to finish, because when you come back to it next time, you'll waste precious minutes wondering where it was you'd got to. Save the 4-hour job for a day when you have the full 4 hours.

150. Never Quit, but a Break is Fine

But I'll be honest with you, some days nothing works, and you'll wonder why the heck you even started.

Then it's best to take a break and go do something else for a while. Get out of the house, visit a friend, or go for a walk; do something fun or relaxing.

151. Recognise Your Limits

Importantly, you should learn to recognise what stuff tests your limits or pushes you close to your breaking point. For me it's boring, physically hard stuff like digging etc. (yes, I'm getting to be a wuss in my old age!). Factor these things into your plan if need be, maybe you could arrange some help for those parts, (i.e. I'll provide the food and beer, you just bring a shovel...).

"When you reach the end of your rope, tie a knot in it and hang on."
Thomas Jefferson

152. Always Think Ahead

Never walk away from the workplace empty handed. Think about what stuff you've finished with. Pick it up and take it out as you go, even if it's just a piece of rubbish. This will save a dedicated trip out with it later.

Conversely, never walk towards the workplace empty handed either. Is it possible to take the tools/material/etc. into the workplace for the next task? Be methodical in your actions and less... erm... random! Paint in a logical sequence for example, not waving your arms about like a man flagging down a bus...

153. Batching Saves Time

Combine all similar tasks into one batch and tackle them in succession. Every time you stop and change direction/tool/task, you lose time. In your plan group the same tasks together logically if possible.

Efficiency is intelligent laziness

154. The Two-Minute Fix

Consider keeping a couple of screwdrivers somewhere handy (in a kitchen drawer?) so you can employ the 'two-minute' rule' where anything taking less than two minutes or so to fix, you deal with on the spot.

This way you don't get behind on jobs, but it does require good discipline...

155. Some Thoughts about Caulking

It doesn't matter if you're using silicone or decorators caulk these tips will help...

- Do all your preparation work first because you cannot sandpaper caulk in any way.

- Primer etc. first because caulk sits better on a painted or primed surface (it slows drying out and you get less shrinkage).

- Only buy really good quality caulk, cheap stuff shrinks like heck-a-doodle.

- Treat yourself to a 'heavy duty' caulk gun 10 times better than the cheap ones and good gun doesn't cost the earth.

- Cut the long nozzle at around 45 degrees close to the tip.

- Grab a permanent marker and draw a line back from the nozzle tip on the longest side. This helps to correctly orientate the tip when you can't quite see properly.

- For silicone sealant, run a rubber-based tool over the bead at an angle. This takes off any excess and leaves a nice shape bead.

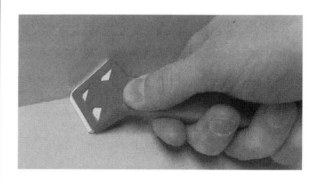

I now use the expensive 'Cramer Fugi' ones, but I've also had good results with the one in the previous image.

- Don't push too hard on the tool though.

It's generally difficult to get a truly flat bead like the left-hand side bead in the next picture, (but that is the strongest).

The one in the middle is what you get mostly, especially if you finish off the bead with a lubricated finger!

Here are the common bead shapes...

Bead Profiles for Silicone Sealant

Most volume of sealant at edges.　　Okay volume of sealant at edges　　Thin volume of sealant at edges, (it can peel away).

For best results, always use a rubber smoothing tool if possible.

BEST　　OKAY　　WORST

- For decorator's acrylic caulk; wet a finger (or thumb) with a damp rag and smooth out the line of caulk, pressing it back to where you want it. Usually as small as possible.

Use the damp rag to tidy up any excess caulk from places you don't want it. Fold the rag over if you've got sealant on it, to avoid getting sealant everywhere. Rinse out the rag every few runs.

- Wipe any excess sealant on your finger onto the top of the gun (to save your trousers/rag etc.), and just cut it off occasionally.

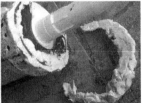

Wait before painting. Overnight is best (even if it says 1 hour on the tube!).

156. Masking Up

I'll be honest with you, for many years I didn't use masking tape. Being young I thought, (dare I say it), it was strictly for amateurs! Oh, the ignorance of youth. Then I discovered 'blue masking tape'.

Blue tape is way better than regular tape. If you don't have a 'blue' masking tape in your neck of the woods, ask the guys in the store for a low tack tape which can be left in place for a few days and you'll probably end up with something very similar.

Some masking tape tips then...

- Clean the place you're going to stick the tape. A very slightly damp rag works well (and let it dry afterwards).

- You must, must, must press down the very inner edge of the tape. And I don't mean run your finger along it, because (unless you've got very weird fingers) the round end of a finger will not get right onto the edge. Gently and lightly run your thin, flexible paint scraper or putty knife along the very edge of the tape where the paint will go to seal it onto the surface.

- On narrow trims (skirting boards etc.), leave the tape sticking out to better protect the trim from paint splatter from a roller.

- Tape over holes. It's difficult to paint over holes without getting runs as the paint comes back out of the hole. Simply put a small square over the hole and paint right over it.

- Run a lightly loaded paint brush up to and onto the tape a little way. Never, and I mean never, run a fully loaded paintbrush onto the masking tape, as you'll end up with thick, dried paint in the corner and the tape will be very difficult to remove cleanly.

- Before removing masking tape, run your paint scraper gently along the edge of the tape to 'break' the paint in the corner.

- Store the tape in a bag or box. If you chuck a roll of blue masking tape, (or any tape really), into your bucket of tools, the edges of the roll get bashed, boshed, binged, and... i.e. buggered.

157. Don't be in a Hurry to Put Things Back

If you have removed stuff prior to painting around them, do wait a while before you put them back. Paint stays soft for quite a while and if you put stuff back too soon it'll stick and make taking them off next time difficult. Minimum 48 hours for most paints, and a day longer than that is even better.

This also applies to closing stuff like doors and windows etc. Or anything where there is contact with the fresh paint.

158. Commit to Producing Quality Work

Producing great work comes from not compromising your craft...

- It's about following good working practices.

- It's about not leaving something out because it's inconvenient or because you want to finish quickly.

- It's about using the right fasteners or the right tool for the application.

- It means going back again and again, making small adjustments until it's perfect.

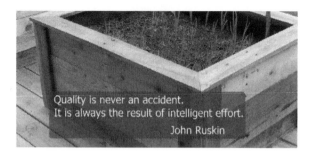

Quality is never an accident.
It is always the result of intelligent effort.
John Ruskin

- Lastly, it's having the resolve to stop, abandon that particular piece and start all over again, if that's what it takes to get it right.

PREPARATION AND PLANS

"planning is bringing the future into the present so you can do something about it now"

Alan Lakein

159. All Projects Need Planning

In lieu of experience you need a plan, because a plan will encourage you to think through each part of your project.

You'll discover what you need to buy and what you need to learn. In short, it'll help you with the details.

160. A Simple Plan Consists of...

Just three things...

- A list describing the project plus your notes, (overview).

- A list of what you need, (preparation).

- A list of what to do, (planning).

161. Don't Delude Yourself When Planning

Go wild with your plans for sure, (they are free after all), but be realistic. Don't make grand plans for your garden if (in reality) you

know you'll only have time to sit out there on the odd warm evening in the late summer.

Consider having low maintenance areas, rather than gently winding paths though elaborate flowerbeds and water features.

162. Find Out What You Really, Really Want

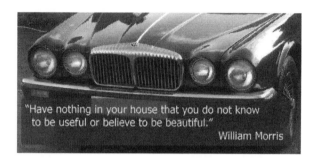

"Have nothing in your house that you do not know to be useful or believe to be beautiful."
William Morris

And unless you're a Spice Girl, it's not going to be zigazig ah. So, before deciding on your improvements, consider the following...

- How do you use the different spaces day to day? e.g. where do you eat, hang out, relax, store stuff, washing requirements etc.

- How does your use of space change in the evenings or at the weekends? Flop on the sofa for a movie and pizza or beers you're your mates in the garden etc.?

- How does your space fit all of your entertaining needs?

- Are you using all the area you have, or are there 'dead' areas that are underutilized or even places you never use?

- What about your storage needs, is there enough? Stupid question, there is never enough.

- Are you storing stuff you never use? (Recycle, give away or sell it!).

- Do you struggle or get frustrated with anything? If so, think about why and what you'd need to fix the problem.

- What are your furniture needs? Breakfast, daytime, night time, evenings, entertaining, inside, outside etc.

- Are there enough power outlets and are they in the right places? (err, never!).

- Is there enough lighting? Think about mood, placement, and different situations (cleaning, reading, guests etc.).

- Is your space practical? How do you handle rubbish, laundry or firewood, workshop space, is there an 'out of sight' working place in the garden etc. for all your practical or working stuff?

- How do your needs change throughout the seasons?

- Do you have enough outside space, storage, parking, etc?

- The garden? Oh, there's always more to do in the garden!

163. Always Keep Good Records

Always keep records on file for any bigger home improvements, especially stuff like extensions, new kitchens or bathrooms, new heating systems or any structural work, inside or out. It might be important one day to know exactly when you removed the chimney or when you fitted the new hot water tank. Store everything from receipts to guarantees and even your own notes about the job.

Any official paperwork related to permissions etc., from the local authority obviously gets pride of place in this file. Everything will be interesting and useful to you and even any future owners.

164. Before Spending Cash in the Garden

The first step is, as usual, to get to know what you already have in your garden and how it works. Think about the 'soft' stuff first...

- Which direction does the sun come from?

- Note the shade and full sun areas as they change throughout the day on a rough sketch of your garden.

- Note any dry or damp areas on your rough sketch too.

- Note any 'frost pockets' or cold spots in the winter time.

- What soil do you have, acid, alkaline, sandy, loamy, clay, rubble, rocky etc? Cheap testing kits are available or search online for "soil testing"; the BBC gardening and RHS are great for advice.

- Are there any special factors that affect your garden, wind, sea air, high rainfall, low rainfall, heavy snow etc?

- The above points will help you choose suitable plants for each area. All plant labels have symbols to indicate what conditions they like to grow well.

- Garden use; how do you use the space? Do you sit out relaxing a lot? Or do you like to be busy in the garden working with plants etc? Or, do you just enjoy looking at it out of the window because you're busy?

- How much time do you have for maintenance & upkeep?

- Do you go away often? Choose plants that can cope with dry conditions unless you have accommodating neighbours or can afford to install complex automatic watering systems.

- Always make sure you design a planting scheme that fits your lifestyle.

- As a shortcut, look at what are neighbours are growing? Copy planting schemes when it's clear they are thriving.

- Ask for small cuttings to get free plants if your neighbours are friendly. Steal them when they are on holiday if they are not... (just kidding...).

- Google 'seed swaps' or 'seed exchanges' in your area to get cheap or free seeds close to home (and to meet interesting people).

  and then think about the hard stuff...

- What are your parking space requirements, and will they change when any children get older etc?

- Do you hang washing outside to dry? A line or a carousel?

- Do you entertain in the garden or cook outside regularly?

- What seating requirements do you need?

- How much hard standing area do you need in relation to the soft-planted areas? Do you need landscaped pathways to access all areas?

- What storage space do you need for garden tools, lawn mowers and other gardening paraphernalia etc?

- Do you need a greenhouse or cold frames or space for planted cuttings or seedbeds etc.?

- Do you have space for a small vegetable garden, (or large if you're fortunate)? You should, you really, really should you know, you'll love the end results...

- What storage do you need for any outdoor pursuits like bicycles, skis, sports equipment, and sledges etc?

- What other storage space do you need for stuff like trailers, caravans, or if you're lucky, a motorbike or a boat etc.

- Incorporate a small area screened from the general garden at the side of or behind a well-positioned potting shed for example. Use it for your compost heap (in the sun if possible), spare bamboo canes, wheelbarrows, water barrel, new cuttings, etc.

- And for those of us in colder climes, you'll need to think about snow; or more specifically, where to put it!

165. Always Have a Plan B (just in case)

Since you never know what you might find or what might happen, especially with an older house; it's essential to have a list of folks to call 'in case of emergency'.

Get to know a plumber, electrician, or a builder etc., before you start. As usual, ask your friends and colleagues for a reliable contact in each trade.

Don't, whatever you do call random guys from the local phone book or classifieds, especially when you are vulnerable in an emergency.

Plan B consists of calling any good guys you hear about, or better still make an appointment to see them in person; perhaps you could call in and visit them on their current job?

Then just introduce yourself, (tell them who sent you and say that you've heard nice things about their work etc!)

Briefly tell them what you plan to do and if it's okay for you to call them and hire them for a short while to help if you get stuck.

Paying someone to come for an hour or three to avoid struggling with a problem is just smart; everyone needs a helping hand occasionally.

166. If You Don't Know Any Locals

If you're new to an area and don't know anyone; go to the local builder's merchant during a quiet time of day (not first thing, lunchtime or at closing time) and ask at the counter for a recommendation. Or ask to see the sales representative, these guys are always looking to talk to new customers.

Sure, they might all joke and say 'no-one, they're all useless around here!' but then listen to what they say.

Trust me, these guys see everyone and know exactly who the good guys are, or more importantly the guys to avoid.

Always ask with a smile, or better still chocolates...

167. Half and Half

Consider doing the time consuming (but less technical) parts of a job and then hire in a specialist to finish off the more skilled parts.

Call in your friendly plumber for a quick site visit to talk through what's needed. Then get on with the 'donkey work' like chopping holes in walls and running pipes etc (plastic is brilliant!). Once the pipes are all in, back comes the plumber to fit all the expensive, complicated bits.

Do the same with your tame electrician, chopping holes in walls, drilling holes through floor joists, fastening the backboxes, forming cable runs and even running cables.

You could cut and fix all the drywall and then hire in a busy plasterer just to do the finish plaster (skimming in the UK) or tape and fill the joints.

You could wash down the paintwork and sandpaper it all up ready for the painter to work their magic with a brush, (although that sounds pretty boring, I'd rather hire someone to wash down the paintwork and sandpaper it all up ready for me to paint it!).

Consider hiring in some muscle for any heavy lifting. Remodelling the garden and afraid of the heavy materials? Local teenagers are always looking to earn cash, hire one to bear the brunt of the heavy stuff.

BUYING STUFF

"The fellow that owns his own home is always just coming out of a hardware store."

Kin Hubbard

168. Who Sells What?

Familiarise yourself with your local stores and what they sell. Collect leaflets and brochures. Take photos of things with your phone and when you get home, use the photos to search for the brand names you saw to find loads more info online.

169. Material Quality and Compromise

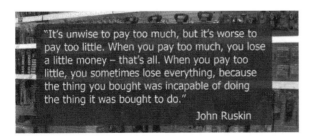

"It's unwise to pay too much, but it's worse to pay too little. When you pay too much, you lose a little money – that's all. When you pay too little, you sometimes lose everything, because the thing you bought was incapable of doing the thing it was bought to do."

John Ruskin

Before setting a budget remember that the price you pay, the quality you receive, and how long it all lasts, runs along a sliding scale of compromise. Mass-produced, budget quality stuff has a limited life expectancy, whereas well designed stuff made from high quality materials could last generations. Some clever clogs once said, 'If you buy quality, you only cry once', he was right.

170. Choose Carefully

Someone once said that 'tomorrows antiques depend upon your purchases today'. Food for thought...

"Good design doesn't date."

Harry Seidler

Great design with solid engineering, backed up with good quality materials is a winning combination. For example, the watch above has coped with more than twenty years of working in a heavy construction environment, including years in hot and dusty Africa, and yet it thrives.

I anticipate giving this watch to my son when I'm gone, I'm that confident in its strength. Prior to this, I used to buy watches costing about a day's wages and they'd all fail within a couple of years or so.

171. Handling and Transport

Getting heavy or awkward stuff into the car or trailer without damage often needs two people (tip, take a friend or don't be shy, ask a passer-by). Don't rely 100% on the packaging to protect stuff either, a piece of cardboard or polythene isn't going to stop you scratching your new door if you slide it over the tailgate latch or a stone in the bottom of the trailer. Take extra padding (blankets, sheets, foam etc.).

Obey the rules for specific loads, for example fridges and freezers don't like it if you lay them down, but if you can't avoid it, stand them the right way up for a day or so afterwards before switching them on. Washing machines will have transport screws which you must remove before use etc (and put back if you move, so keep them!).

Oh, and some good straps to tie down properly.

Always go under the roofrack bar and back over the material. Bring any loose ends back on itself and under the bar again to prevent it coming undone. Wrap any spare length around the load or tuck it into the vehicle and close the door on it. Strap beats rope every time.

Learn how to tie stuff down properly with decent straps (rope is hopeless unless you know how to tie the truckers hitch...). Knowing where to tie is quite an art form and it's vital you do it properly. Even then, it's a good idea to stop after driving for a few minutes, just to double check everything is still secure. Sometimes stuff moves after a few pull offs, corners and braking etc. (go easy on corners and try to avoid heavy starts and braking etc.).

Carrying thin sheet material is especially difficult. Thin stuff on a roof rack or sticking out of a trailer is prone to snapping under the wind load of driving.

Try to get a curve in the sheet, which adds strength. Put a length of timber in the middle of the roof rack for example and strap the sheet down over it.

This is especially important if you have a loaded roof rack or towing a heavily loaded trailer. Distance doesn't matter, always secure stuff properly.

If you lose part of your load or even if the load is too heavy for your vehicle or trailer, your insurance will be invalid.

If you lose something from your vehicle or fail to stop in time in an emergency, because your vehicle is overloaded and you hurt someone (or worse) you're in trouble, and I mean a lot of trouble. Like, 'go-straight-to-jail-and-don't-pass-go" kind of trouble.

172. Build Relationships with Suppliers

No, I don't mean take them out to dinner. I mean 'be cool', don't be unreasonable in your dealings with them. And in turn, they'll support you, every day with good service.

Plus, it'll only cost you a big box of chocolates come Christmas, some friendly banter day to day and never being inconsiderate (i.e. insisting on 'no notice' last minute deliveries).

Building a relationship with a supplier is like any relationship though; it will have its ups and downs from time to time. Deal with any problem politely, getting angry will just make future purchases difficult and embarrassing for everyone.

You want staff to smile when you walk into a store, not run for cover muttering 'oh no, it's that fool again'.

173. Buying Timber

If you see a timber stack anything like the one above, just run like mad and head to another store.

Store timber properly supported along its length with good air flow to avoid problems.

Seriously, you'll find nothing but pain buying timber from a place that keeps its timber in unruly stacks like this.

174. Always Select Your Own Timber

Because of this variation in quality, always select your own timber, even if you're having it delivered by the store. Because there's always the chance when you order it over the phone that some of this 'rejected' timber will find its way into your delivery.

175. Sort the Good from the Bad

The above is a pretty normal example showing some savvy person rejecting timber (piled on the left) by sorting through the stack to select good quality lengths to take away.

You should definitely do the same...

176. Take a Long View

When you sight down a length of timber, bring one end up close to your face and look down one side, turn the piece through 90º and look again. You should clearly see any defects as the eye is a great 'instrument' for detecting curved things or anomalies.

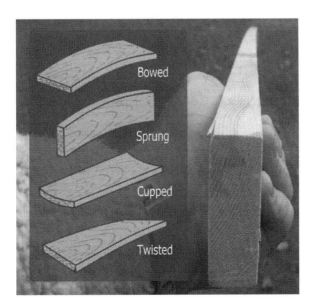

Bowed

Sprung

Cupped

Twisted

177. Don't Worry About Bends (unless diving)

The 5mm 'cupping' in this piece means it's best avoided.

Bends (or bows to be pedantic) are less troublesome than twists or cupping across the width. A slow curve in a timber is easy to straighten out on fixing, but twisted or cupped timber is difficult to flatten without splitting it.

178. Store Timber Properly & Ahead of Time

Got wood?

Once you get your timber home, store it on several supports under and in-between it to allow warm ambient air to circulate around it. It's best to have it close to where you're going to install it and in similar conditions (same humidity and temperature). Acclimatising timber can take from a few days right up to a couple of weeks

Don't stick it in your unheated garage for two weeks and then use it in a room at 23ºC because you'll likely have a problem with shrinkage.

179. There are Only Two Sorts of Timber

There are two groups of timbers; Softwoods which come from evergreen, needle-leaved, cone-bearing coniferous trees, such as pine, cedar, and fir trees etc.

Then there are the lovely broad-leaved, deciduous hardwood trees which drop their leaves each autumn, such as ash, beech, birch, mahogany, meranti, oak, sapele and teak trees etc., beautiful trees all.

180. Three Finished Timber Products

Rough Sawn square edged timber with a sawn finish straight from the sawmill, used for framing and roofing etc.

CLS (Canadian Lumber Standard), the smooth round cornered timber used for building internal 'stud' walls or framing. Often lighter and kiln-dried for optimum use internally. Don't use this outside.

Planed Squared Edge (PSE or its close cousin PAR, planed all round) smooth planed timber used for frames, trims, and finer work.

181. How Strong is Your Timber?

Timber is visually strength graded (and sometimes machine graded) at the mill to look for natural growth characteristics which might adversely affect strength, including knots or unusual grain slope, for example. For construction use C16 is the most common. The likely usage of the timber by size, will dictate is quality; timber suitable for floor joists for example will be a slightly higher grade, C24 usually. Higher grades such as C30 (and higher still) are available for especially highly stressed situations.

182. Odds, Ends and Other Useful Stuff

Odds, ends and all manner of potentially useful things.

If you're smart, you'll start saving 'odds & ends'; i.e. stuff that might 'come in handy one day'. This stuff every handy person should have in 'stock' to enable you to find creative solutions on future projects.

Save leftover materials and fasteners from your own projects, accept donations from other people (who aren't as smart as you) plus you can reclaim useful things from stuff you send for recycling.

183. Some Stuff Worth Saving...

- Leftover timber offcuts or any clean timber from stuff you've dismantled / taken down.

- Leftover fixings and fasteners, bolts, screws, nails etc.

- Leftover new materials, either for future repairs or for new projects.

- Fixtures, fittings, brackets, cables, and other useful materials stripped off anything going for recycling.

- Plastic sheeting for protecting stuff in storage, protecting floors during decorating or even in the garden to smother weeds etc,

- Large bits of cardboard are useful to protect floors or other work surfaces from damage when using tools etc.

- Old fabric/ clothes/ etc. make good rags in the workshop.

- Old sheets, curtains etc. are useful for covering down (dust sheets).

- Empty paint tins or glass jars make great nail pails or useful storage containers for small odds and ends.

- Metal stuff. Save a few pieces or sections of scrap metal to use when you need to fabricate something.

184. Big Brands vs Home Brands

Good quality tools made by leading manufacturers will make you feel good every time you look at them (let alone use them), whereas poor quality 'home brand' tools will make you cry every time you pick them up.

185. Don't Buy Tools from Dubious Sources

Please be careful where you buy second hand tools from.

The theft of tradesmen's tools has reached epidemic proportions. And in my humble opinion, if you buy stolen tools, you're as bad as the thieves...

Don't be shy in asking the seller why they are selling or where they are from. If they want to know why you're asking, tell them. Tell them you're just being careful because you don't buy stolen tools because that is just plain wrong.

186. A Good Starter or Minimum Tool Kit

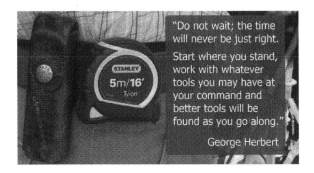

"Do not wait; the time will never be just right. Start where you stand, work with whatever tools you may have at your command and better tools will be found as you go along."

George Herbert

The following is a good basic tool kit, the ones you'll probably use the most, your every-day tool kit if you like.

- A selection of different screwdrivers (slot, Pozidriv, Phillips, TORX).

- A claw hammer (16oz is great, or 20oz if you're a farmer...)

- A club or lump hammer (2.5 pounds or about 1kg is fine).

- A small wrecking or crow bar. The flat types are good.

- Cold chisels for masonry, 13mm (½″), 19mm (¾″) straight chisels and a 75mm (3″) bolster. Oh, and you'll need gloves for these...

- A set of wood chisels for, err... wood. 10mm ($^3/_8$″), 13mm (½″), 19mm ($^3/_4$″), 25mm (1″) will cover most jobs.

- A new hardpoint saw for timber.

- A hacksaw for cutting metal (junior or full size)

- A pair of pliers.

- A sharp craft knife.

- A small nail punch.

- A flexible paint scraper.

- A carpenter's square.

- A bunch of pencils.

- Oh, and something sturdy to store them all in. As a minimum use a big rubber bucket or a tool bag. Better still is a big tool chest.

187. What About Power Tools?

There is lots you can do with hand tools alone, but a mid-sized (14V) cordless drill driver will be very useful and if the budget runs to it, also get a mains powered SDS drill which will drill holes in anything (wood, brick, blocks, and concrete etc).

Maybe a jigsaw would make a good power tool No. 2.

After that the sky is the limit...

188. Hiring 'Expensive to Buy' Tools

Need a tool for a one-off job? Instead of buying a cheap 'throwaway tool', consider hiring a professional quality tool. They're more powerful, quicker, more effective and you'll find it easier to achieve a high-quality finish.

Plus, it's difficult to justify buying any tool if you're only going to use it once in a very long while. Tools you'll need for fitting a kitchen for example.

Hiring tools saves capital investment and frees up storage space, plus you'll always have the latest tools and technology.

It also gives you another person to ask for advice, especially since it's likely to be the first time you've needed that particular tool (don't worry, they are used to it!).

Don't forget to ask for the safety literature and any 'how to' leaflets they might have.

FIXINGS, FASTENERS AND HARDWARE

Fixing describes the whole process (e.g. join the timbers together with a metal strap) and the fasteners (in this case) are the nails and the hardware is the metal strap.

189. How to Choose Screw Length

Sometimes screw length is automatically restricted because of the thickness of the timber you're fastening together. Screwing two pieces of 20mm (¾″) stock together for instance, where you'd use 35mm (1 ¼″) screws.

Usually you'd aim for a screw length of approximately two and a half to three times the thickness of the material you're fixing (your workpiece). For example, to fix a 20mm (¾″) thick timber batten to some framing, you'd use a 50mm to 60mm (2″ to 2 ½″) screw.

190. End Grain Always Needs More Length

If you're screwing into the end grain of a piece of wood (down the grain) instead into the cross grain (90° to the grain) allow a little longer length because end grain doesn't hold a screw thread very well (when compared to cross grain).

Always be especially careful to drill good pilot holes as end grain splits easily if the screw gets too tight.

One tip is to drill larger holes into the end grain and glue in a dowel. Then drill the pilot hole in the dowel, ergo the screw will be in cross grain. Clever, those old chippies!

191. Choose Your Screw Drive System

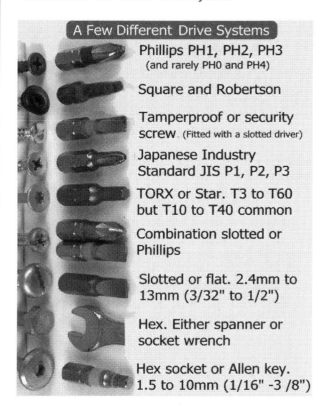

192. SOME COMMON SCREW HEADS

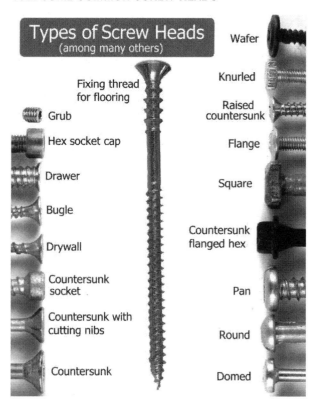

193. Choosing Screw Gauge or Thickness

The length of the screw gives good support against pull out forces but in most cases the load is in 'shear'. This where the weight or load is across the screw and here it's the gauge or thickness of the screw which carries the load.

Light loads = smaller gauges like 3, 4, 6 & 8's (2.5mm to 4.0mm) are ideal for small lightweight stuff and lightly loaded things. Heavy loads = heavier gauges like 10, 12 & 14's (4.0mm to 6.5mm) ideal for bigger, heaver stuff or things expected to carry large loads.

194. Go as Big as You Can with Fasteners

Often the size of the holes in most hardware (brackets etc.) indicates the gauge of the fasteners you should use; i.e. use the thickest gauge fasteners you can get into the holes.

195. Crikey That's Tight my Dear

Never use brute force to drive in screws, because once they get too tight the tip of the driver will twist out of the screw head, (called 'cam out)', and will damage the screw head and even the screwdriver tip. Stop, take it out and drill a bigger pilot hole.

196. Installing Screws: Tip One

Drill a pilot hole in the timber you're fastening into. Make it the same diameter as the screw shank (minus the threads) or a tiny bit less. This makes getting screws in easy and won't split the workpiece.

197. Installing Screws: Tip Two

If fastening together two pieces; clamp them together and drill the above pilot hole through BOTH pieces.

Then unclamp and drill a clearance hole (the same diameter as the screw) though the top piece only.

This prevents a nasty thing called 'jacking', where the two pieces don't pull up tight to each other because the thread is cutting into both pieces.

198. Installing Screws: Tip Three

If you want your screw to sit flush with the top, then make a shallow countersink hole in the top piece (you can start with this if you want). Most softwoods don't need this as they are soft enough for the screw head to pull into anyway. MDF or Oak, not so much.

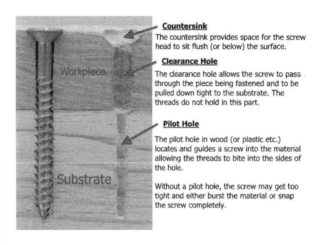

Countersink
The countersink provides space for the screw head to sit flush (or below) the surface.

Clearance Hole
The clearance hole allows the screw to pass through the piece being fastened and to be pulled down tight to the substrate. The threads do not hold in this part.

Pilot Hole
The pilot hole in wood (or plastic etc.) locates and guides a screw into the material allowing the threads to bite into the sides of the hole.

Without a pilot hole, the screw may get too tight and either burst the material or snap the screw completely.

199. Don't go Too Deep, It's Not Better

Many sheet materials (think particleboard, chipboard, MDF and the like) often have a harder wearing surface and are softer in the middle. The tightest hold is when the screw head is exactly flush with the board top (where the board is hardest). Screw heads sunk deep into the softer middle part of chipboard for example, don't hold nearly so well.

200. Don't Create a Water Pocket

Related to the above. Especially leave all external and especially decking screws flush with the surface.

If you sink these deep into the wood, water soaks into the torn timber fibres forming the depression, (rotting the timber and corroding the screw itself).

201. Removing Difficult Screws: Tip One

If a screw is too tight to move, stop before you damage the screw head and try a short sharp tap or two on the end of a firmly held screwdriver with a mallet (it's okay, I know you'll use your hammer...). This often 'breaks' the hold the material has on the threads.

Follow this up with a LOT of downwards pressure (perfectly in line of course) with your screwdriver or drill driver on slow and 'pulse' the trigger to have a fighting chance of removing it.

202. Removing Difficult Screws: Tip Two

If you've got good access, cut a slot into the damaged screw head using a hacksaw or Dremel type tool. Then tap in a big slotted screwdriver and remove the screw.

203. Removing Difficult Screws: Tip Three

A long shot is to try a rubber band or even fine sandpaper, (grit side down) underneath the screwdriver tip. As above re: the high pressure needed (it's a long shot though).

204. Removing Difficult Screws: Tip Four

Use a special 'screw extractor' which digs into the damaged head and drives it out but to be honest these will not always work and often end up snapping the head off smaller screws.

205. Can't Get a Screw Out: The Last Resort

Using a small drill bit of say 3 or 4mm (⅛″) drill down all around the sides of the broken screw, through the first part of the material. Pull off the top material. Remove the screw that's left sticking out of the substrate with a pair of pliers or mole grips.

OR.

Use a hollow, small diameter core drill and likewise drill down and around the broken screw, (I've even seen a bloke do this with a short length of metal pipe!). Be very careful when starting up, because without a centre guide drill bit, the core drill bit will try to walk all over the workpieces surface (I did say this is difficult!).

Repair both the above large holes by drilling out and gluing in a short piece of dowel to replace the damaged area.

206. Lag Screws for Heavy Jobs

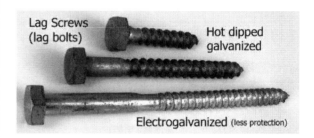

Lag Screws (lag bolts) Hot dipped galvanized

Electrogalvanized (less protection)

Lag screws (or bolts) are like a bolt only with a large screw thread at the end rather than fine threads and a nut. Be careful not to overtighten lag screws or you'll strip the relatively soft threads in the wood (because the tightening force of a spanner greatly exceeds a screwdriver).

Lag screws are not known for their pull-out properties particularly, but more for their enormous shear strength due to the huge gauge. This makes them a first choice for things like heavy brackets etc.

You'll need to drill two holes to fit a lag screw, a clearance hole in your workpiece to clear the solid part of the shank and a pilot hole in the substrate, for the threaded part to screw into.

207. Construction or Structural Screws

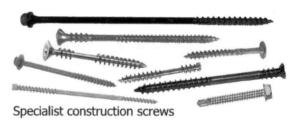

Specialist construction screws

For bigger connections. Construction screws often have self-drilling tips plus deep, coarse and sharp threads to make driving them deep into big timbers easy. Big threads like this also hold extra securely, which is important on big joints.

There's also some rather nifty double thread screws which have virtually no head because the holding power comes from threads at the top and bottom of the fastener; available in tiny sizes for secret screwing of floorboards up to large sizes for construction joints between large timbers.

208. Frame Fixings for Doors and Windows

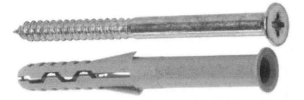

The screw and plug are the same length, so you never 'lose' the wall plug as you install both plug and screw from the front. Drill a hole through the frame, then swap drill bits and drill the substrate (usually masonry). Blow or vacuum out the dust.

Loosely insert the screw into the plug and push/ hammer the whole thing in until the plug is flush with the frame; tighten as normal.

You'll need to insert packing in any gaps between the frame and substrate (commonly plastic spacers.

209. Use Wall Plugs in Masonry

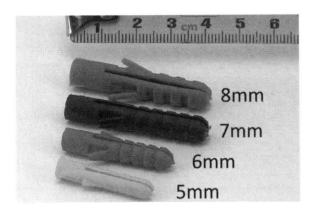

Wall plugs are just wedges pushing the two halves of the plug apart and filling the hole very tightly. Friction then takes care of holding everything in place for all eternity; it's handy stuff friction... and best of all, it's absolutely free!

It's very important the whole length of the plug is in the actual substrate; brick, block, stone, concrete etc. (and not in any weak plaster etc.).

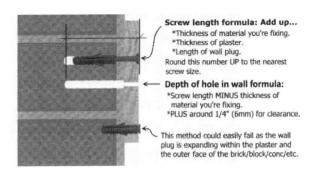

Screw length formula: Add up...
*Thickness of material you're fixing.
*Thickness of plaster.
*Length of wall plug.
Round this number UP to the nearest screw size.

Depth of hole in wall formula:
*Screw length MINUS thickness of material you're fixing.
*PLUS around 1/4" (6mm) for clearance.

This method could easily fail as the wall plug is expanding within the plaster and the outer face of the brick/block/conc/etc.

210. When Wall Plugs Don't Work

When wall plugs are too loose, (in poor or soft substrates like old crumbly bricks or blocks) glue them in place. Clean out the hole (important!), then using a 'no-nails' type tube adhesive, squirt a small amount as deep as you can get the nozzle into the hole.

Then push in the wall plug and use something blunt to push the plug into the adhesive and down to the right depth.

Wait 24 hours (I know, it's a pain, but what can you do!) and then try again with the screw.

211. How to Make Emergency Wall Plugs

When wall plugs run out after the inevitable zombie apocalypse, improvise by using; matchsticks, cocktail sticks, thin slivers of wood, or even chopsticks!

Tap as many as you can get into the hole and snap them off flush with the surface. It's an ideal tip for oversize holes where a screw has stripped its threads.

For added strength you can dip them into wood glue first, before putting them into the hole.

212. Use Expanding Anchors in Concrete

Anchor holes range in diameter from 6mm (¼") up to around 24mm (1"). Lengths range from 45mm (1 ¾") or so up to 190mm

(7 ½") or so. Typically, though, you're probably going to use an M10 (⅜") or M12 (½") anchor going into the substrate 75mm (3") or so.

Heavy Duty Expanding Anchors

Expanding shield anchors

Throughbolts

Sleeve anchor

Installation of expansion anchors is virtually identical to the plastic wall plugs mentioned above with one exception. You MUST clean out the hole after drilling. This is because the holes are much larger and therefore hold much more drilling dust which will interfere when you try to insert the anchor and tighten it up.

You need to get these anchors right first time, because if you get stuck half way in, they are near impossible to remove.

213. When to Use Resin Anchors

Resin anchors are an alternative anchoring system developed for high loads in difficult locations such as...

- Close to the edge of the substrate, where a conventional expansion anchor would likely crack the substrate.

- Softer materials, such as lightweight, ash or clinker blocks, certain soft or flaky stone, soft or crumbly bricks etc. where expansion anchors wouldn't be able to get a firm grip.

- Hollow substrates such as any brick with holes or frogs or blocks with voids etc.) where there is nothing for expansion anchors to push against to develop a friction grip.

- An alternative method when you need deep, very secure anchors, such as in rock etc. (think rope bridges, climbing anchors etc.).

Resin is ideal for all substrates though and gives absolutely immovable rock-solid anchors (groan, excuse the pun!). Basically, it's a threaded bar glued into the bottom of a hole and up top there's a washer and nut to hold the object down.

There are several resin systems. Some involve pushing a fragile capsule filled with resin to the bottom of a hole, followed by the threaded bar which breaks the capsule and mixes the resin components. More common is a two-part tube with a clever spiral nozzle which mixes the two-part resin as you squirt it directly into the hole, followed again by the threaded bar. In hollow or crumbly substrates insert a special plastic sleeve first which helps the resin stay in the right place and not run into the voids (there is nothing worse than being in the void...).

The holes are typically a few mm's (⅛" or so) oversized to allow space for the resin. This means you'll need to support the threaded bars to keep them in the position you want (otherwise they will sag to the side or bottom of the hole, possibly at an angle (especially if on a vertical substrate).

214. I Want a Long Run of Stuff on a Wall

Consider fastening timber rails or battens to the wall (screwing into the studs behind the drywall) and then fasten stuff to the rails. IKEA's new kitchen cabinets for example, now utilise a slim metal rail which you screw to the wall along its length and then the cabinets hang from the rail. This system gives maximum flexibility to find good fastening points.

215. Hollow Wall / Drywall Fasteners

Choosing the right fastener to hang stuff from drywall is all down to weight, as the fixing depth often remains the same i.e. the thickness of the drywall (or occasionally double thickness, for which fasteners are also available).

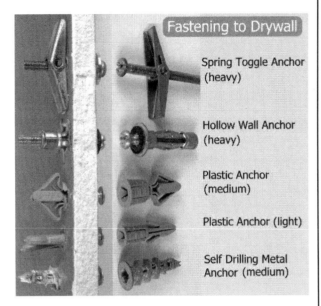

Each class of fastener will handle a certain amount of weight before 'pulling out', with or without a chunk of drywall.

You'll find a guide for the holding capacity of a drywall anchor clearly marked on the packaging.

216. I Want to Hang Heavy Stuff on Drywall

I'd recommend finding the timber framework behind the drywall and getting some longer regular screws into the timber for good measure (if at all possible). This is a good idea especially for big TV brackets etc.

217. Planning Ahead for Heavy Stuff

Incidentally if you're building new stud walls and you know where heavy stuff is going to be in advance, add extra timber noggins between the vertical studs so you have a solid block of timber to fasten stuff too. I always build in 50mm × 200mm (2″ × 8″) blocks of timber (floor joist offcuts) at 900mm or 36″ high (worktop height) and at 2m or 6′ 8″ high (top of kitchen cabinet height) which makes installing kitchen units a breeze because you

can then just screw straight into the wall using regular wood screws.

218. How to Choose Nail Heads

The type of material, plus the load it's going to carry, dictates the shape of the nail head.

Big loads mean decent sized heads (and long length and heavy gauge). Small loads mean tiny heads. Fragile material might need oversized heads to prevent tearing through, roofing felt nails for example.

Round bright wire nails with medium sized round flat heads are the most common for general framing and joinery. 50mm (2″), 75mm (3″) and 100mm (4″) are popular.

Lost head or finish nails (where the head is only minimally bigger than the gauge) are common for general finishing work where you don't want to see big ugly nail heads. Nail these in close to the surface and finish off by using a nail punch to punch the nail slightly below the surface (to protect the surface of your workpiece from your hammer). Popular sizes are from 38mm (1 ½″) up to around 75mm (3″) or so.

Oval nails are in the middle and ideal for medium sized trims like architraves etc. Always orientate them with the long oval along the grain to minimise splitting.

Panel pins are small versions of the lost head nails suitable for small trims. From 12mm (½″) up to around 50mm (2″) or so in both bright steel and lightly galvanised or sheradised (which is just a fancy way of saying 'dry galvanised'), or even copper or stainless steel.

219. How to Choose Nail Length

As with choosing screws, choose your nail length based on the thickness of the timber you're fastening together. Nailing two pieces of 20mm (¾″) stock together for instance, where you'd use 35mm (1 ¼″) nails.

Ideally though, aim for approximately two and a half to three times the thickness of the material you're fixing to. For example, to fix a 20mm (¾") thick piece of timber to some framing, you'd use a 50mm to 60mm (2 to 2 ½") nail.

220. Some Common Nails from my Box

Common Nails

Bright round wire nails. General framing and construction. Size 25mm to 150mm (1" to 6"). Common sizes 50mm, 75mm and 100mm (2", 3" and 4"). Various gauges. *

Lost head nails. Barrel type head is ideal for face work and is easy to punch below the surface. Size: 25mm to 100mm (1" to 4"). Common sizes 50mm and 65mm (2" and 2 1/2").*

Annular ring nail. Great for sheet materials. Size 40mm to 100mm (1 1/2" to 4"). Common sizes are 50mm, 65mm and 75mm (2", 2 1/2" and 3"). Difficult to remove.*

Galvanised clout nail. Small sizes have large heads ideal for roofing felt. Larger sizes make good general purpose nails for indoor and outdoor work. Size 13mm to 75mm (1/2" to 3"). Common sizes 20mm, 25mm, 38mm and 50mm (3/4", 1", 1 1/2" and 2"). Also available in copper for fixing slates.

Oval wire nail. Ideal for finish carpentry as their shape means less likelihood of splitting. Small heads. Size 25mm to 100mm (1" to 4"). Common sizes 40mm 50mm and 65mm (1 1/2", 2" and 2 1/2").*

Square twist nail. Used on joist hangers and straps. Superior holding power and thick gauge. Size 30mm and 40mm (1 1/4" and 1 1/2"), both common.

Square cut or clasp nail. Stamped out of flat metal. Old style suitable for nailing floorboards or into light weight blocks. Large holding power. Size 50mm 65mm, 75mm and 100mm (2", 2 1/2", 3" and 4"). Common sizes are 65mm and 75mm (2 1/2" and 3").

Masonry nail. Very hard nail for nailing into hard substrates like brick and concrete (in theory). Sizes 25mm to 100mm (1" to 4"). Common sizes, no idea, I hate the blooming things and never use them...

Panel pins. Thin, narrow head nail perfect for fixing trims and thin panels. Sizes from 13mm to 40mm (1/2" to 1 1/2"). Common sizes are 25mm and 32mm (1" and 1 1/4").*

Galvanised staple. Used to hold wire and mesh. Size from 15mm to 40mm (5/8" to 1 1/2"). Common size 25mm (1").

Tacks. Carpet and upholstery use. Very sharp point and large head. Sizes from 10mm to 25mm (3/8" to 1"), all common.

*These nails are available galvanised for outdoor use.

221. Try to Avoid Nailing into End Grain

If you can, avoid nailing into the end grain of a piece of timber (down the grain), because end grain doesn't hold nails very well. If unavoidable (and it often is), be especially careful not to split the timber.

Drill small pilot holes if you need to (mostly on smaller timbers) and use longer and thinner gauge nails than normal if at all possible.

222. Choosing Nail Gauge or Thickness

As with screws, the gauge or thickness of the nail depends on the weight of the item you're fastening, plus the expected load it's going to carry. Small lightweight stuff and lightly loaded things like trims etc. don't exert much pull on their fasteners so thin nails are fine.

Once you start going up in timber size, the load or weight and pull on the fasteners increases exponentially. Medium weight things like fascia boards, or large skirting boards need nails in the middle of the gauge range. Save the heaviest, thicker gauges, for larger stuff like framing or fencing etc.

223. When to Use Cut Nails

Cut or clasp nails, made by stamping them out of flat sheets of thick metal, are a bit of a throwback to earlier times. Being oblong in section and having blunt ends, plus a small 90º angle at the top, they have great holding power. Used to hold down floorboards in the old days, but now useful for nailing into light-weight blocks funnily enough (a real mixture or old and new tech!). Handy also to create that period look...

224. What About a Power Nailer?

So, the powered nail gun. Once the pre-serve of only the most handsome of carpenters, is now available to everyone. Even my daughter's been using one since she was 13, (under supervision of course).

Collated air Nails

Mechanical nailers come in several forms now; with gas or battery powered nailers replacing the traditional compressed air. The new generation of battery-powered nailers are ideal for DIY use as there are no airlines to get in the way or struggle with.

Nailers deliver nails decisively, accurately and with just enough force for the job. Just ensure you're using the right length and gauge (thickness) nails for the size timber you're nailing. Don't expect thin 18g trim nails to hold 50mm × 25mm (2″x1″) battens and conversely don't use 75mm (3″) clipped head nails to fix your architraves, because it won't look pretty...

Oh, and safety glasses are essential when using mechanical nailers, seriously, don't even think about it.

225. How to Join big Timbers Together

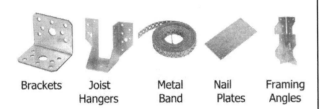

Brackets   Joist   Metal   Nail   Framing
         Hangers Band   Plates   Angles

Traditional joints such as the 'mortice and tenon' are rare and nowadays big timber joints usually involve a selection of proprietary metal to timber connectors. There is one for just about every occasion and they're most commonly found supporting floor joists or in roofing applications.

Today the range is so big you could build almost anything with them, from a dog kennel to a timber framed house.

Most timber connectors require special, strong nails (or occasionally screws) to fix them in place. Regular fasteners might not be up to the job and could fail.

226. If You Need a Versatile Fastener

Metal banding is handy for general holding and reinforcing jobs such as bracing. Fasten it diagonally across timber walls and floors to create triangles, which as we know from our school days, is the strongest shape

and ideal for bracing or strengthening structures.

Use heavier metal straps to join floor joists to walls, hold down wall plates/roofs or tying gable ends into roofs for example.

Always ensure straps go across several timbers though, fastening to one isn't any good at all. Minimum of three and always add solid timber blocking in between or on top of the joists/rafters etc.

227. Tell Me More About Bolts

Hex Bolts

Hex bolt with plain 'grip length' plus a plain washer and nut.

Fully threaded or tap bolt plus a plain washer and nut.

Bolts consist of a head, a shank, and threads. Tap bolts have threads along their whole length, but regular hex bolts only have threads towards the end.

The plain, non-threaded area on a regular hex bolt is the grip length. The grip length doesn't need threads because it's inside the component or components; only the protruding part of the shank has threads to receive the washer and nut (or to go into threads cut into the last component in the assembly).

228. What About the Threads?

No, not your clothes, these threads are what make your fasteners work. Threads or more correctly screw threads, have two forms; internal and external. Internal threads live inside a nut or component. External threads live on the outside of bolt shanks.

The main types of threads you'll see are...

- ISO Metric*. Standard in Europe and common across the world. Sizes range from M1 through to around M36. Most common sizes range from M5 to M12. Most are coarse pitch by default, but there are fine pitches available for specialist applications.

- UTS Unified Thread Standard. Common in the USA and Canada. Available in coarse, fine, and extra fine...

- UNC (Unified National Coarse).

- UNF (Unified National Fine).

- UNEF (Unified National Extra Fine).

Thread types vary from coarse threads, suitable for general work, up to really fine threads, suitable for screwing into a thin part or a high load application for example. Pitch is the measurement from the top of one thread to the top of the next and ranges from coarse to extra fine.

Coarse threads resist stripping and cross threading better because the threads are bigger and easier to engage. They are also fast to install as they need less turns to drive home.

Fine threads have a larger contact area (because there are more threads) per length of screw, which means they hold better and are less likely to vibrate loose.

However, fine threads are easy to install cross threaded due to the small starting angle and little distance between the threads.

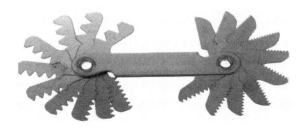

The easiest way to figure your threads out, is to grab yourself a cheap thread gauge which you hold onto the thread in question; keep trying different ones until you hit one which fits snugly, then read off the type of thread on the side of the tool.

229. What is a Left-Hand Thread?

Most threads are right hand or normal, i.e. you turn them clockwise to tighten (remember 'righty tighty and leftie loosie').

But on some rotary objects there is a risk of the rotational force undoing the fastener. In these instances, for the fastener to stay tight, the threads on the bolt must tighten the opposite way to the rotation of the object. i.e. Left-hand threads.

If ever in a situation where a fastener appears to be unfeasibly tight and doesn't want to yield to your tool, take a look at the rotation of the object. If it is clockwise, there is a possibility that the fastener is a left-hand thread so check any threads you can see for orientation.

If they slope from left to right, viewed sideways on then it's left handed and you need to go anti-clockwise to undo them.

You'll find left hand threads on bicycle pedals/cranks, drill chucks, circular saw blade arbours, some left-hand side wheel hubs and so on.

230. How Do I Modify Fasteners?

If you want to shorten a bolt for example, you'll need to protect the threads during the process, as they damage easily. Never hold them directly in the jaws of a vice or grip them with a pair of pliers or grips etc.

Buy some soft jaws for your vice (or make some out of two bits of wood) or try threading a couple of nuts onto the bolt, tighten them against each other, then you can hold the nuts tightly (steady now!) in the vice instead. This will protect the threads as you cut the bolt with your hacksaw or mini grinder.

After sawing the bolt, you'll find the end has a burr stopping you from threading on the nut. Using a fine file, create a small chamfer all around the newly cut end which should restore the startability (made up word) of the nut. Another way to ensure a clean end is to thread on the nut first, cut the bolt and then take the nut off. This should clean up the last thread, but it's still best to tidy up the end with a file.

231. Can I Hit Threads with a Hammer?

Another thing about threads. Never, ever hit them with a metal hammer. Ever. Tempting though it is to try and tap out a stubborn bolt, if you hit the end thread, you'll never get the nut back on again, ever.

Always unscrew the nut until it's protecting the end of the bolt and then hit the nut. Oh, and even then, it's best to use a soft faced hammer. Hide and copper combination hammers are common (but heavy plastic ones work okay too). Copper etc. being softer than steel, it should dent before causing any serious damage to the steel threads.

232. Nuts and Bolts: Tip One

If there is space, always use a socket before a spanner, they have more control and you can exert more force with less chance of slipping (which almost always results in losing some skin off your knuckles).

233. Nuts and Bolts: Tip Two

Obvious, but always use the right (and I mean exactly right) size socket/ spanner etc. It should be a good fit. If you can move the socket head or spanner handle left and right more than a fraction, it's the wrong size.

234. Nuts and Bolts: Tip Three

Always apply the force at exactly 90° to the fasteners shaft. The wrench head (even if it's cranked slightly) must sit perfectly flat and down around the nut or bolt head. If one side is even slightly lifted up, it will slip under force (and skin your knuckles).

235. Removing Difficult Nut or Bolt: Tip One

Sh*t happens, and nuts and bolts corrode, it's as simple as that. First try soaking it with a penetrating fluid (like WD40) and walk away for a while. Go get a cup of coffee, walk the dog, or just sit in the sunshine and ponder the mysteries of the universe. When you get back the fluid will have miraculously sorted out the problem, no?

236. Removing Difficult Nut or Bolt: Tip Two

As we looked at earlier, the first thing to try is to apply more force...

Two spanners doubles the turning force...

Or slide a long metal tube over the handle to increase the turning force. Be careful though, as you'll soon reach or exceed the breaking point of the fastener. If the fastener is that tight you might want to think about using shock or heat (tips 59 and 60).

237. It Started Okay, But...

Occasionally a fastener will start to undo okay and then become tight after a few turns. Always wire bush rust off any protruding threads if you can see them. Alternatively keep working the fastener back and forth as you undo it to clear any rust off the threads (i.e. out half a turn, back in a quarter of a turn, repeat). This method stops the rust building up and wedging the threads.

Really tight fasteners also become hot and expand (not helping matters at all), use WD40 as a coolant and lubrication.

238. The Floor is Dirty; My Mummy Said So

And she was right. There's no 'two second' rule here. Never put fasteners on the floor. Always pop them into a receptacle of some kind to keep them both clean and safe. I use a variety of empty plastic tubs such as ice cream tubs (plus you get to eat ice cream...).

Don't forget to thoroughly clean any dirty or dropped fasteners before re-assembly, grit on threads is a nightmare. A wire brush and degreasers are useful here.

239. Copper Grease is Made in Heaven

Related to nuts and bolts, don't forget when working on older machines that a smear of copper grease is beneficial when re-assembling most kinds of fasteners. It prevents corrosion and thus makes disassembly easier during future maintenance.

240. Crossed Threads are Really, Really Bad

Your worst nightmare in fact. Always be 100% sure the fastener has started properly before reaching for tools.

Crossed threads are where the threads on the fastener don't align properly with the threads in the nut or worse still, in the component. Instead of following the existing threads, the male part (e.g. the bolt) tries to 'cut' a new way into the female part (e.g. the nut or part), quickly getting very tight or breaking or stripping the threads inside.

Particularly common where there are different materials involved, i.e. a steel bolt going into an aluminium component.

First, pop the bolt or screw back into the top of its hole and gently turn it anti-clockwise as if you were undoing it again (or clockwise for rare left-hand threads). You will feel a small 'click' as the thread on the fastener (bolt for example) drops over the thread in the hole (in the nut for example). Once it clicks, gently start turning the fixing in the opposite direction, (tightening it).

Second, keep going by hand as far as possible, because it's near impossible to cross-thread a fastener by hand (unless you're a meta-human...). If it becomes tight early, stop, and investigate why.

241. How Tight is Tight Enough?

In most cases, run up a fastener until what's called hand tight and then either turn it a further part of a turn with a tool. Large fasteners in hard metal might only need a further $\frac{1}{8}^{th}$ of a turn to fully tighten. But a small fastener in a soft metal like aluminium, well, you're in the 'tighten by experience' zone and you'd be better off using a torque wrench set to the specified setting.

The 'tightness' required to hold something in place is specific to the size of the fastener and the load it carries. Stuff that's heavy, fast moving or vibrates, need to be very tight indeed. Stationary or lightweight or small things obviously don't need to be so tight.

242. Always Clean First and Then Lube

Two things you need to do, especially on old nut and bolts. First, it's very important to clean up any dirty or rusty threads with a wire brush and under the bolt head. Second, I like to use a lubricant on old bolts. Both of these reduce friction, enabling you to properly tighten them up.

243. Always Hand Tight First, Then Tools

As we looked at above, in general it's best to get all the fasteners in place and hand tight first, before reaching for a tool. If you tighten one all the way, it often makes getting the others started difficult, increasing the risk of cross threading.

244. Opposites are Best

On stuff with multiple fasteners it's wise to tighten them in a logical pattern. For example, replacing a four-bolt car wheel (replace wheel with a multi fastener item of your choice). First pick a bolt (or nut) and tighten it up until it's just snug, preferably by hand, or with the socket in your hand (from the socket wrench) for a little added leverage (hand tight). Then do the same to the bolt opposite. Then you have a choice of bolts (left or right), but the point is to move around the wheel/ component working on opposite sides each time. This helps settle the wheel (read component) in exactly the right place with no distortion.

245. What are Washers For?

Washers have two closely connected jobs; first, a washer spreads the compression load exerted on the component by the action of tightening the nut or bolt. Second, washers make it easier to tighten the nut by reducing the friction between the underneath of the bolt head and the component. Without a washer, the rotating edge of the nut could score and dig into the workpiece. Instead the washer provides a kind of slip plane between the component and the nut making it easier to achieve the correct torque.

246. What is Shake Proof Stuff For?

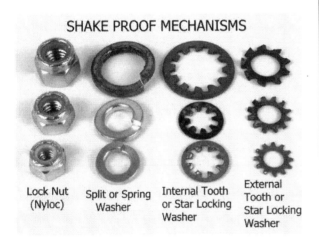

SHAKE PROOF MECHANISMS

Lock Nut (Nyloc)   Split or Spring Washer   Internal Tooth or Star Locking Washer   External Tooth or Star Locking Washer

Stuff that moves will vibrate, and vibration, in theory, can lead to a nut rotating, undoing it gradually over time. To combat this, you'd typically use either shake proof washers or shake proof nuts.

Shake proof or lock nuts (NYLOC being the most common) have a little plastic insert right at the top of the nut (often blue) which grips the threads tightly. It's advisable to replace shake proof nuts with new ones every time they're removed, especially on anything

with a critical safety function (they are cheap). Ordinarily though, if you're working on your wheel barrow, it might not matter so much, but always use new ones on the Ferrari...

To stop regular nuts shaking loose, use a special shake proof washer in conjunction with a plain or regular washer. Fitted in between the plain washer and the underside of the nut a shake proof washer digs into the metal on both sides, holding them in place.

247. Why Use A Thread Locking Compound?

Use a thread locking compound (Loctite being the most famous) when there is a risk of high vibration. The compound is essentially a glue (of varying strengths) which, on contact with clean metal fasteners and in the absence of air sets into a hard plastic. Because the compound fills the gaps between the threads it locks everything up and as a bonus helps prevent corrosion (no air or water you see?). Different manufacturers use colours to denote different strengths and you'll most commonly see blue (medium strength) and red (higher strength).

Thread locking does make components more difficult to remove, as that is kind of the point. But not impossible; (some of the highest strength compounds might need heat to soften them). Generally, you'll still be able to undo nuts and bolts treated with Loctite using regular tools, they'll just be a bit tight to start off with, you might even need to 'shock' them loose with a good pull on the wrench to 'crack' the seal the compound makes with the metal.

Clean up the threads with a wire brush and wipe off with a rag. On re-assembly, add a small amount of the compound onto the threads before either inserting a bolt or stud into a component or a nut onto threads.

248. What are Starlock Push on Fasteners?

Starlocks are retaining washers, push on washers, or just push nuts. Commonly used to hold small wheels on to shafts, like those found on prams, pushchairs, strollers, sack trucks and lawnmowers etc., or to stop a shaft from moving around or coming out once it's gone through a component.

Starlock Push On Fastener or Push Nut

249. How Do I Remove a Starlock Washer?

They hold in place by spring loaded prongs; effectively one-way barbs which makes them tricky to remove.

Because starlocks are considered single use (they are very cheap to buy) you'd normally remove them by cutting the outer rim with side cutters and twisting them away. Replace with new ones. However...

250. What if I *Have* to Use a Starlock Twice?

Alternatively, if you must save an original, the trick is to lever up the little prongs against the shaft itself to relieve their grip, one at a time. A pointed pick, a very small flat screwdriver or a tiny pair of needle nosed pliers will do the trick, work each prong up a little at a time going around and around them all. This should work the starlock washer up the shaft, eventually freeing it.

Sometimes, if you lever up one or two of the prongs you can almost un-screw them like a nut to get them off.

Don't lever the whole washer up around the outer rim, because that makes them dig in even more (unless the shaft is plastic, then the prongs will dig in and reverse direction allowing the starlock to come off at the expense of a little damage to the plastic shaft).

Some starlock washers have a cap or decorative dome which covers the prongs. Unless the dome cap pops off, you might just have to lever the whole thing off and hope for the best.

Removal usually damages starlocks, although if you're careful and take your time, you might get away with it, especially on something not particularly stressed like a toy pram etc. If you insist on re-using the old ones, straighten out the prongs a little with a small hammer before re-fitting.

251. How do I Fit Starlocks?

Ensure the prongs are sloping upwards and install new starlocks (or good reclaimed ones) by tapping them into place using a suitable sized hollow tube. I find a suitably sized socket from a wrench/socket set works just fine. There are of course special tools for the job, although you'd probably have to order one online.

Dome style starlock washer to hold a sack truck wheel

The dome styles often have a rim around the edge for fitting. If not try a piece of rubber or leather under the tube (to protect the thin dome).

Don't tap the dome with a hammer (however tempting it is), you'll dent the dome, guaranteed. The ones pictured previously I managed to push on with my big thumbs...

252. How Do I Fasten Big Timbers Together?

Bigger structural timbers, such as those in a roof, utilise bolts to form structurally strong triangle shapes.

You can buy special timber bolts which are ideal to hold big stuff together. Having large domed heads, timber bolts only need one tool as the head side looks after itself due to some clever spurs on the underside of the head.

Some folks use regular coach bolts for bolting timber, but the small square on the underside of a coach bolts head should really go into a metal part (a farm gate hinge strap for example or a large metal washer with a square hole) to stop the bolt turning as you tighten the nut.

253. Aren't Timber Bolts Expensive?

For general assembly of timbers not normally seen, (smaller roofs etc.) you could use threaded bar, a cheaper alternative to special timber bolts (but cutting it up takes a little time).

Simply cut threaded bar into short lengths and assemble with washers and nuts both ends. However, bear in mind that threaded bar may not be as tensile/strong as regular coach bolts, so check with your structural engineer first if you're bolting really large or particularly stressed timbers. Use very large washers to prevent the bolt head or nut pulling into the timber under load.

254. Why do I Need Dogs, I'm a Cat Person?

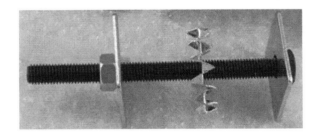

Not that kind of dog! To improve all bolted joints in timber, use dogs or 'dog toothed timber connectors' (their proper name) in between the timbers, to resist sliding forces. You can even use wood glue here, both methods add a huge amount of strength to the joint.

ASSEMBLING & INSTALLING
(FLAT PACKS ETC.)

"A child of five would understand this. Send someone to fetch a child of five."
Groucho Marx

255. Isn't Flat Packed Stuff Hard?

Nah, arguably, the manufacturer has done most of the hard work for you. Self-assembly stuff is simple enough for 'anyone to do' by design; i.e. this stuff is specifically *designed* for you to assemble. For anyone who can pick up a screwdriver actually, and some bits don't even need the screwdriver!

Flat pack assembly is an ideal starting point for you to start figuring out how things go together and to try out those new tools. So quit ya whingin' and let's get on with it.

256. The 8 Unbreakable Rules of Flat Packs

1. Clear your working area of clutter before opening any boxes to create the best workspace possible (why struggle?) oh, and to avoid losing any of the small parts, (you'll need ALL of them!).

2. Identify and familiarise yourself with each component as you remove it from its packaging (be observant!). Learn the terminology for each part as you check it off the packing list.

3. Put all the small components into containers etc. so they don't get lost. Use a separate container for each package until you're more familiar with the parts. When doing kitchens, we dump all the small stuff into one of the drawers.

4. Read the instructions (yes really!) and keep them close for frequent reference during assembly. Afterwards, file them properly so

you don't lose them, just in case, (well, you never know...).

5. Check fasteners are in the right holes, lots of flatpack stuff is modular (used on multiple things) which means not all the holes will apply to your build. Holes look similar, so double check the instructions.

6. Take care with alignment; double check parts are in the right place and pointing in the right direction.

7. Take care with fasteners or fixings to avoid crossed threads. Always start and run them up by hand where possible. Applies to nuts going onto bolts and tap bolts going into threaded holes.

8. Especially don't over tighten fasteners in chipboard, particleboard or MDF, as it's very easy to ruin the threads. Stop as soon as you hit the surface and it has pulled up with no gap.

257. Seriously, Read the Instructions?

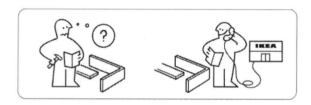

Yup, I really mean it. Not reading instructions properly is the number one reason folks make mistakes.

It's almost like there's a mental troll sitting in the brain saying, 'proper handy people don't need instructions' (The same guy who stops you from asking for directions when you're lost).

But the truth is, you're wrong! Professionals like me fit so many new, 'never seen before' things, that reading instructions becomes a must and plus, it's a perfect excuse for a paid coffee break...

So please, I implore you, grab yourself a coffee and READ THE INSTRUCTIONS from end to end before you start and then keep referring to them page by page during the build.

I know, I know; it goes against all popular reasoning for a person to read the instructions *first*, instead of waiting until you get stuck. Nevertheless, reading instructions is essential, if you want to master the flat pack game and avoid an 'out of sequence assembly' which is like having an 'out of body experience', i.e. something to avoid at all costs...

However, be warned, you will sometimes need to be patient with poor instructions and persevere. Sometimes you'll need to actually start the job and read them page by page before the instructions make sense. Or, try reading them out loud, it really does help sometimes (seriously!).

Pay particular attention. if something has a choice of 'hands', i.e. something can be on the left or right etc. *Always look at the image at the top of the page first*, sometimes you need to jump forward to a particular page to assemble the thing exactly how you want it.

258. What's the Point of the Packing List?

An often-ignored part of the instructions is the packing list of parts at the front.

Use this list of parts to teach yourself the names (or reference numbers) of all the parts and fixings used in the build (and what they look like), because it will save you time during the actual assembly.

Most importantly, it stops you using the wrong fastener. Getting the wrong fastener will either break something (if it's too long) or trip you up during a later part of the assembly (if it's too short).

Good instructions (like IKEA) will show you what fastener not to use as well as the actual one to use (with reference numbers).

259. What is a Dry Run?

If you're not sure how something fits together or you don't quite understand the instructions, try what's called a dry run.

Fit the parts together without glue or fasteners. Sometimes just holding the parts up allows the brain to figure it out in a way that it just can't see on paper.

This really helps you to visualise what you're building and will help prevent mistakes. Once you confirm the parts fit together properly with no problems, go ahead for real.

Dry runs are especially helpful if the assembly includes glue or sealant for example. It's horrible when you apply glue or silicone to everything and then realise that you've forgotten something, or it doesn't quite fit and you end up with rapidly setting gloop all over the place. Messy.

260. Overcoming Discrepancies

In an ideal world, everything would be flat, level, plumb, square, and true, unfortunately, stuff built by the lowest bidder on a tight price and even tighter schedule, rarely meet that ideal.

Before you start, find out if there are any discrepancies where you're working. Knowing which way a floor or wall runs out of true, may give you an advantage later in the job. Usually, the older the house, the more aware you need to be about discrepancies, but new houses are not immune to errors either, so always check first.

Straightedges (or a long piece of straight timber or string line), spirit levels and a big square are your best friends here. Poke them everywhere and take note of anything they highlight, look for gaps, dips, hollows, bulges, out of square corners, out of level, out of plumb etc.

Measure discrepancies and ensure there is enough adjustment in what you're working with to cope with how out of true the location is. Running out of adjustment backs you into a corner and there might not be an easy solution, in other words, you're stuck.

Each job is as unique as its discrepancies and once you've identified them, you'll need to really think them through and ask, "will this affect what I'm doing?".

Think about how to get over the discrepancy and get the job to still look good. Maybe it's best to start in a particular place, a low point, or a high point, left or right or even in the middle! Maybe you need to add material to correct an area before fitting your new stuff (think extra plaster in a hollow area on a wall or a little 'self-levelling compound' in a dip on the floor).

Maybe there is a way to hide the problem or cover it up (think trims, cover strips, end cover panels etc.). Maybe you need to remove material to correct a problem, an outward bump or curve in a wall where you want to put a new kitchen worktop for example (think, remove a little plaster).

261. When There is No Room to Build in Situ

Sometimes you have no choice but to assemble something in one area (space constraints usually) and then move the finished article into its final place for fitting.

Bear in mind that rough handling may seriously weaken the structure of many self-assembly things, because they are just not designed to cope with those kinds of stresses.

Two invaluable tools are the sack truck, which makes moving things easy, even heavy things like washing machines. Simply slide the thin blade underneath, tip the item back until the weight is balanced and wheel it wherever you need to go. The other tool is a wheeled trolley. These are flat boards with castors at each corner and come in various sizes. Simply lift the item onto the trolley and wheel into place. Ideal for heavy things like pianos and other things that are too heavy or big for sack trucks.

262. No Sack Truck? Use a Bed Sheet

No really. You can move quite heavy items by lifting them up one end and laying a sheet underneath them. Lift up the other end and pull the sheet through so it's totally underneath the item.

Then simply grab good handfuls of the sheet and pull. The whole thing will slide easily on the sheet. BUT, you must make absolutely sure the floor is super clean and grit free if its wooden. Carpet, nah, not so much.

THE SIMPLEST MAINTENANCE TOOL KIT IN THE WORLD

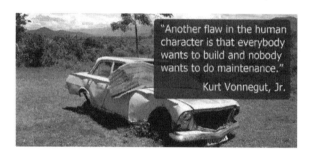

"Another flaw in the human character is that everybody wants to build and nobody wants to do maintenance."

Kurt Vonnegut, Jr.

I rather like the 'duffers' tool kit, which consists of a roll of tape and a can of WD40. The theory being; 'If something moves that shouldn't, you tape it up, and if something doesn't move, but should; you give it a squirt of WD40.' Although intended as a joke, when it comes to maintenance, it's actually pretty close to the truth. A little goes a long way in maintenance.

263. The Basic Principle of Maintenance

It doesn't matter whether you're maintaining a vehicle (bike, scooter, motorbike, car, van, boat etc) or a wardrobe; the basic principle is the same. You carry out maintenance to preserve conditions and counter wear and tear.

The biggest enemy of your stuff is neglect, because neglect eventually turns into failure. Then simple maintenance no longer works and you're looking at repairs.

The trick to learning how to maintain something is to have a very basic understanding of how the components look and work.

Don't worry, you don't need to know the science, just think about...

- Is this supposed to move, (yes/no or is it stiff/free)?
- How does it feel (the same or different)?
- What vulnerable parts do I need to protect from corrosion or wear?
- Is that supposed to happen (catch/rub/wear etc.)?
- What needs replacing regularly (parts, paint, etc.)?

264. The Five Basics of Maintenance

1. Keep stuff clean (dirt, grit, dust, and tired lube are bad).

2. Lubricate vulnerable moving parts (lubricate and be free!)

3. Make timely adjustments to stuff starting to wear (a few little tweaks go a long way to stave off failure).

4. Replace service parts (service parts are designed to wear out over time to protect delicate or more expensive parts).

5. Maintain finish integrity (rust, rot & oxidisation are bad).

Keep on top of small maintenance jobs because they are easy and cost little. Ignoring any of the above leads to little problems, which over time turn into bigger problems and eventually, complete failures or breakdowns. The longer the interval between maintenance checks the larger the final bill for repairs.

265. But I Hate Cleaning Stuff

Keeping stuff clean isn't just about making stuff look pretty though, (although it does), but more importantly, cleaning removes the grit and other contaminants held in the build-up of muck (lubricants especially attract and hold dust and grit).

This gives your stuff a real reliability and longevity boost because tiny abrasive particles like grit increase friction, impede performance and cause components, surfaces and finishes to wear out prematurely.

It's especially important to clean stuff before applying any new lubricants, otherwise you might push the aforementioned congealed contaminants and abrasives further into the working parts (not good).

Cleaning also means getting up close and intimate with your stuff, you'll spot anything unusual or amiss very early on. You might notice a small, hardly visible malfunction; wear marks on a component or some tiny damage to a finish.

266. Use WD40 as a Mini Pressure Washer

WD40 is a fair cleaner and it comes in a pressurised can. Use the thin tube to blast out old lube, grit etc, on a small part or a bicycle chain for example, wipe off and then re-lubricate with the recommended light machine oil.

Don't try this on anything sensitive!

267. Let Chemicals Do the Work

Hard work used to be the preferred method of cleaning, but today, there are many different chemicals to do much of the scrubbing for you.

Bearing in mind the desired end result you want, study the applications, or uses on the packaging of the product to ensure it's suitable for your project (you can really damage stuff if you get this wrong). You can always double check with store staff if you need something, especially symbols, explained in more detail. The store might also have additional technical sheets, especially related to using the product safely (many strong cleaning chemicals will burn skin and eyes).

Although the blurb on some packets might claim the product is a simple spray on and rinse off process, this is rarely the case and a good soak does wonders with nearly every cleaner, reducing 'elbow grease' dramatically.

Spraying on a cleaner and then immediately attacking it with a brush wastes effort and chemical. Agitate the chemical well into the gunk with a brush for best penetration, repeating several times for even better results. Don't forget, old toothbrushes are great for cleaning small or intricate stuff.

The exceptions to the above are the more powerful or acid-based cleaners, which are time sensitive. Reading the manufacturer's instructions is very important or they may remove more than you bargained for. Always protect your eyes and any exposed skin when using powerful acid cleaners.

268. How do Lubricants Work?

Lubricants do much more than you think...

- **Friction and wear**: If moving parts were to touch each other, friction would quickly wear them out. Lubricants keep moving components separate (even if it's microscopically) and prevent wear to individual parts by reducing or eliminating friction.

- **Cooling**: Friction also builds heat as you know, and lubricants soak up this heat carrying it away from vulnerable components. The oil in an engine is a great example, it's not there just to lubricate, it acts as a coolant too.

- **Cleaning**: lubricant attracts debris such as particles from the surroundings and microscopic particles created by wear This debris degrades the lubricants quality and is why lubricants need replacing from time to time. Engine oil turns from a golden honey colour to black goop for example.

- **Corrosion**: lubricants are great at preventing corrosion by excluding air and water from the oxidising reaction.

- **Sealing**: lubricants help seal against air and water finding their way into places where they'd cause damage. Smearing petroleum jelly (Vaseline) onto a hosepipe O ring for example, not only helps facilitate repeated coupling and uncoupling, it will protect the seal making leaks less troublesome. Lubrication also helps seal gas or air tight fittings.

- **Power**: lubricants are incompressible, making them ideal to transfer power via hydraulic action. Telescopic rams on construction equipment or the fluid inside a vehicles automatic gear box etc.

Be aware that some components have self-lubricating parts (due to special materials), and yet others are sealed for life, so check the manufacturer's information first.

Before replacing lubricant, first, you'll need to remove any existing lubrication (i.e. drain old engine oil or use a degreaser to remove old lube).

Also, any lubricant filters (think engine oil filter), need replacing, thus removing any contaminants they contain.

269. What Lubricants Should I Use?

Visually check any lubrication points or moving parts to try and identify what type of lubricant is already there (consult the original maintenance documents if possible or search online).

Choose the same or similar specification (grade) lubricant for best results. Generally, slower moving things need thick lubricant like grease and faster moving things need thinner and high-performance lubricants (for their stickiness and stability under extreme conditions).

Be vigilant for any signs of stiffness, creaking or squeaking from any moving component, a sure sign the lubrication has dried out completely. Any seized component, (e.g. moving parts that don't) needs attention immediately or you risk other components breaking because of the extra stress the non-moving part adds.

Here's a few of the most common...

270. WD40

WD-40 is the 40th attempt to make a Water Displacement chemical and is very useful for lots of jobs. WD-40 has five basic properties:

- **Cleans**: WD-40 helps to dissolve dirt, grime, and grease. It also dissolves adhesives, allowing removal of labels etc.

- **Displaces moisture**: use it to get rid of damp in electrical systems to eliminate moisture-related short circuits.

- **Penetrates**: WD-40 loosens rust-to-metal bonds and frees stuck, frozen, or rusted metal parts.

- **Lubricates**: WD-40 is a light lubricant suitable for moving parts.

- **Protects**: WD-40 protects metal surfaces against rust with its corrosion-resistant ingredients

271. Light Machine Oil

Light machine oil is a thin, almost transparent oil, that has many uses around the home and garden, lubricating tools, hinges, nuts & bolts, firearms, bicycles, wheels, fans and sewing machines (remember the saying "running like a sewing machine"? Light machine oil is responsible.

It's highly refined and very thin, it gets into tiny spaces ensuring free movement. It's so thin you'll need a rag when using it; apply a drop or two, work the mechanism and then wipe away any excess dripping down. Repeat as necessary. 3-in-one is one of the most famous brands.

272. Regular Engine Oil

Engine oil is a heavier, often golden coloured lubricant available in many grades to suit different operating conditions. Although primarily for inside engines, engine oil makes a good all-round lubricant for many moving parts and is handy to have in the workshop in a little pump action oil can.

Available in two broad types, organic or mineral and the more modern synthetic oils. Oil is measured by its viscosity when cold (w means winter) and when hot, hence the two numbers on the packaging e.g. 20w50. The 20 in this case wouldn't be very good for a cold engine in a cold climate, it's too thick and could impede starting and cold running. 5w40 would be better. The second number is the viscosity of the oil in a hot engine and needs to be higher to allow for the thinning that oil undergoes when heated.

However, used engine oil is a dangerous chemical cocktail and needs recycling safely, although some old timers swear by it painted onto rough metal stuff to stop corrosion.

That may be useful if you own a tractor which lives in a field, but don't try it underneath a sports car which lives on your drive...

273. Copper Grease (anti seize compound)

Copper grease is a thick, very sticky, shiny copper coloured (unsurprisingly!) lubricant. Apply it to bolt threads when reassembling components as it prevents future corrosion and seizing (making future maintenance easier).

Sometimes known as anti-seize compound. Also commonly used sparingly on the back and edges of vehicle brake pad back plates to reduce squealing.

Copper grease copes well with high temperatures and sticks like the proverbial stuff to a blanket, making it ideally suited for moving parts.

274. Regular Grease (lithium usually)

Grease is a thick (often yellow looking) lubricant to protect against wear of moving parts on machines. Often called high melting point grease.

Grease is made from oil mixed with special soap, which makes it very sticky. It's ideal for fast moving components like bearings, but also for slow moving components like, levers on machines, rotating parts, slides, and contact points like door latches etc.

Apply grease directly to the parts, operate a few times to work it right in and wipe away any excess.

In addition, you might see grease nipples on some machines. Grease nipples (Zerk or Alemite fitting in the USA) allow you to easily push new grease directly into a bearing etc., using a special, (but cheap to buy), grease gun.

Grease Nipple (UK) or Zerk Fitting (USA)

Pump new grease into bearings via the spring loaded ball bearing at the tip

Simply wipe the nipple and the nozzle on the gun clean, push the nozzle onto the grease nipple and pump (check the machines instructions for how many strokes) or until it oozes out of the bearing or vent hole.

275. Dry Lubricants

Some moving parts would gum up over time, due to the accumulation of dust and debris sticking to wet lubricants. Things like lock cylinders for example. Your key needs to go in and out of a lock without getting all greasy every time. Enter dry lubricants. Old school (and still pretty good) is graphite (yup, the same stuff they make pencils out of) which is super slippery and ideal for inside dry mechanicals. Don't add graphite to anything previously greased though or you'll make a nasty black paste (thoroughly clean it with a degreaser or solvent and let it dry before switching to a dry lubricant).

Modern dry lubricants are a little more complicated than pencils though. Look out for the word MOLY (short for Molybdenum disulfide).

Plus PTFE (short for polytetrafluorethylene) or for brand names like Teflon, a slippery material you'll already know about from non-stick pans.

There is one last dry lubricant (for humans!) that you might have forgotten about, a surprising one maybe, and that's talcum powder. As anyone who has ever danced on a floor dusted with the stuff or sprinkled it inside rubber trousers will attest. Oops, too much information there...

276. When do I Need a Specialist Lubricant?

You'll find all sorts of special lubricants in this bunch, maybe even one or two that you'd not thought of as lubricants...

- Silicone based lubricant for rubber seals, O rings, washers etc.

- High temperature lubricant for hot environments (it doesn't thin or run in high heat applications).

- Cold temperature lubricant for cold environments (it doesn't thicken and go stiff in conditions of extreme cold).

- Long life lubricant for difficult to access components or where you need a long service life.

- Food grade lubricant; designated safe to use on food processing machinery.

- Edible oils. Stops food sticking to surfaces during the cooking process itself, (think cooking oils etc.) as well as actually a foodstuff in itself (think olive oil etc.).

- Skin safe lubricant which don't harm sensitive skin or other areas; think lip balms, hand creams, sunscreen and other erm, let's just say... more intimate, personal lubricants, (I say, steady on!).

277. How to Get Rid of Old Lubricant

Degreasers. We use degreasers all the time in the home from washing the dishes to cleaning dead flies off car bumpers. These light detergent-based degreasers are fine for general cleaning of lightly soiled surfaces or parts; but there are more industrial degreasers out there, designed to shift even the most stubborn grease or old lubricant.

Often solvent based for spraying onto greasy surfaces or in liquid form for dipping smaller parts into. Follow the instructions carefully as some are powerful enough to damage surrounding finishes.

Some of the solvents you have lying around (like petrol, alcohol, various spirits, lighter fluid etc.) are also brilliant for removing grease, but they are very flammable and dangerous, so you really shouldn't use them; but if you must, ensure you have good ventilation and be careful not to spill any. Oh, and if you do screw up and burn your garage down, remember I did tell you not to use them...

278. When to Make Timely Adjustments

The song says, 'nothing stays the same' and this goes for most of the stuff in your life too. Little by little, friction wears away microscopic amounts of material. Eventually this causes stuff to require small adjustments to maintain a proper fit. Even if you properly maintain your stuff, moving parts will still wear down and although lubrication slows the process down considerably, eventually some adjustments are necessary to maintain ideal operation.

Usually you'll need to adjust something for one of two reasons; when something becomes either too loose or too tight. Sometimes this happens together; a loose cabinet hinge for example might make the door rub its neighbour. Unintentional physical contact nearly always causes excessive wear and tear on at least one of the parts affected.

Periodically, or better still, 'as-you-notice', examine moving parts closely and try to determine which parts should move freely, (like the cabinet hinge pin for example) and what should be tight (like the screws holding the hinge for example).

Again, it only takes a few seconds to look at the hinge, turn the screw to pull the door back into line and it's fixed (experiment with the screw, you'll soon see which way it goes to move the door).

279. What Happens When Stuff is Loose?

Loose stuff causes wear in two ways. First, slack parts cause impact damage within themselves as they move around. A loose fastener for example moves around into opposite ends of its hole under load, causing the hole to become elongated.

Over time, this movement compounds, further elongating or damaging the hole until one day the whole thing will tear out of the now much enlarged hole.

For example, the screws holding up the handrail on your stairs will last indefinitely when they're tight. However, when loose they allow the handrail to move around, eventually tearing those screws right out of the wall. This often damages and enlarges the holes making it impossible to re-tighten the screws.

Second, loose fasteners or worn parts increase the range of movement of each part, often allowing parts to collide with other parts. Loose screws in a door hinge allows the door to hit the frame or worse the other door, bad news if it's a pair of glass doors on a bathroom cabinet or shower cubicle for example.

Checking bolts and other fixings for tightness periodically, stops vibration shaking something completely loose (petrol lawnmowers are famous for this).

However, be careful not to over tighten stuff, especially if it's something which repeatedly comes loose. poop

If something repeatedly becomes lose you need to find out why. Look for vibration, catching or rubbing that might be causing stress on the fasteners or look at the way you use the item (i.e. are you abusing it!).

Alternatively, if it's a nut and bolt type fastener, try adding a shake proof washer or try swapping the nut for a shake-proof one.

280. What to do When Stuff is Too Tight

Anything that's tight or a poor fit vastly increases friction and that means you often need to use excessive force to operate the item. Repeatedly forcing something that's too tight can stress the whole construction, eventually leading to seizure or failure. Stuff that's catching or rubbing also wears out much faster.

Maintaining intended gaps between moving parts is vital for long life. If something is tight or catching, find out why by examining closely how it works. Look, listen and feel for catching parts, wear marks are often visible as rub marks in the finish.

Try to determine if it needs lubrication, or if there is debris in the workings (e.g. dirt in tracks) or if fasteners or hardware have loosened or sagged, or even if there is extra material in the way, for example, doors and/or frames swollen from moisture etc.

For example, a door repeatedly pulled or even kicked to close or open it, will eventually become weak at its joints because of the stress caused by excessive twisting. This will eventually damage the frame too, removing paint or even loosening the frames fasteners.

Fortunately, to tighten some screws, adjust a hinge, or plane a little off a door is not too difficult, just look at the gaps between the door and frame to find where it's tight and remove material where the paint shows wear marks until you have even gaps again. You want at least the thickness of a coin all the way around. Make sure the seals are not causing trouble as well (they often dislodge).

Fix tight stuff by either cleaning, lubricating, tweaking adjusters, tightening fasteners, or removing excess material to increase clearance and ensure proper operation.

Make sure the problem is not a symptom of another underlying problem though…

Going back to the door example, if an outside door starts catching in its frame: is it swelling because...

The paint is old or damaged and water is getting into it either from a leaky gutter or poor drainage or excessive splash back from high ground levels etc. Or is it because of loose fasteners or a loose frame etc?

281. What Are Service Parts?

Some things are simply not possible to maintain by just looking after them because they contain parts specifically designed to wear out. It might seem a nuisance, but most service items are there to protect the more expensive parts, thus actually saving you money (in the long run).

Therefore, ignoring or failing to replace service parts makes no financial sense at all. For example, an oil filter and fresh oil for an engine costs peanuts when compared to repairing an engine damaged by an ineffective oil filter clogged with contaminated old oil.

All manufacturers publish instructions regarding maintenance and service intervals for consumable parts. Check your manuals or search online for specific service details for your stuff. Be aware also that not keeping to a manufacturer's maintenance schedule can invalidate any guarantee you might have in the first few years.

In general, neglecting the replacement of service parts will have an adverse effect on the efficiency and performance of a machine.

Some typical service items then...

- **Oil filters** or screens; replaceable paper or cartridge types or clean metal screen types).

- **Air filters** or screens; replaceable paper types or wash out the oiled foam types, add new oil and squeeze out the excess).

- **Fuel filters**; replace at specific timed intervals.

- **Bearings**; some minimally worn bearings might last a little longer if cleaned out and repacked with grease. Once noisy though, it's generally a remove the old bearing and replace with a new one.

- **Brake** systems; brake pads, brake disks, cylinder seals, remove and replace when worn out.

- **Belts** and other drive mechanisms; usually replaced at specific intervals or when broken on non-critical stuff.

- **Seals**; O rings, gaskets etc. replace at specific intervals to prevent failures or leaks in use.

- **Drive**; clutches and other drive plates. Replace when friction material wears away and drive starts to slip and or motion is lost.

- **Bushes**; rubber or plastic isolation parts which cushion parts from one another under load. Replace when movement is excessive.

- **Electrical**; high voltage items need replacement at set intervals due to electrode wear. Includes brushes in motors, spark plugs in engines. Low voltage items such as batteries, replace when ineffective.

- **Tyres**; the tread or surface material wears away and once the built-in wear bars (solid bands or rubber which cross the tread) become visible, the tyre needs replacing.

The next two are not technically 'parts' per se, but still, they protect more expensive stuff and they need replacing periodically, so I'll put them here.

- **Lubricants**; remove and replace. Things such as oil, grease, gearbox oil, transmission fluid, differential gear oil, etc.

- **Fluids**; drain and replace (brake fluid, coolants, hydraulic fluid, etc.). Air conditioning fluid/ gas needs specialist equipment to replenish as it's dangerous stuff, for you and the environment.

282. What's Attacking my Stuff?

The surface of any material is under attack all the time from a wide variety of factors... here are some of the 'enemies'...

- **Water**; including moisture present in air (×2 because it's that bad).

- **Air**; e.g. oxygen and water mean rust on steel and iron.

- **Sun**; ultraviolet radiation causes UV degradation. Also causes thermal instability by expanding coatings and base materials (oh, and sunburn; ouch).

- **Heat**; accelerates many chemical reactions between elements.

- **Cold**; especially below freezing temps. Causes thermal instability by shrinking coatings and base materials.

- **Chemical**; salts, acid rain, oils or sweat from your skin.

- **Physical friction** or movement; accelerates wear and tear.

- **Careless use** causes damage such as scratches, chips & dents.

Once unprotected, (even if only by a tiny bit) most things outside eventually rot, corrode, erode, degrade, or discolour, even so called 'no maintenance' plastic. To guard against this damage, always keep any finishes and coatings 100% intact to protect the underlying material. Plus, it's important to re-apply finishes before the original finish fails completely and starts flaking away or you'll have much more work to do.

All materials react differently to exposure to the elements...

- **Timber** will rot or attract bacteria or bugs which feed on it. Damp wood is a bug magnet (just ask any bug)! Dry wood lasts centuries.

- **Masonry** goes soft and crumbly or spalls.

- **Ferrous metal** containing iron rusts or oxidises extensively because iron oxide is not protective.

- **Non-ferrous metal** such as aluminium, copper, brass, lead, tin, zinc etc. don't rust, but can corrode, discolour, oxidise, or react to other metals. Some oxides are protective, e.g. the green coating on copper.

- **Metal alloys** such as brass, bronze, pewter or stainless steel also don't rust, but can corrode, discolour, oxidise, or react to other metals. Most oxides are protective.

- **Plastic** discolours, degrades, or goes brittle, sometimes this only affects the surface.

- **Rubber** goes hard, perishes and splits.

- **Fabrics** for example can rot, disintegrate, go stiff or tear easily. Think tents, covers, coats, etc.

Most of the above materials have some kind of protective finish that needs maintenance or topping up periodically. Let's take a look at the specific things you can do to a few different materials...

283. Proper Preparation Before Painting

Cleaning, scraping and sanding before painting prevents your hard work looking like this after a relatively short time.

Because preparation is critical, just slapping on new stuff simply won't protect the material, even if it looks good initially. Generally, do this...

- Scrape away any old flaky layers of old paint.

- Clean paintwork with a 'house cleaner' detergent, with a mould killer element if there are green of black spores on the paintwork.

- A bucket of cleaner and another of clean water and a couple of sponges work well indoors. Wipe over with one sponge and detergent and 'rinse' with the other sponge and clean water.

- Outdoors, careful use of a pressure washer to pump cleaner onto the paintwork works well (don't go too close). Scrub with a small brush on a long handle and afterwards rinse everything away being careful with the angle you use (avoid getting water behind anything), mimic how the rain would hit the surface to be safe. Allow plenty of time for everything to dry.

- Sand down the surface, removing any 'shine' to provide a rock-solid base (called 'key') for new coatings.

- Use a suitable primer on any bare areas, maybe even two coats. Lightly sand with a fine sandpaper to flatten again.

- The final sanding grade should be 120/180 grit (or finer) otherwise the scratch marks may show through the final finish.

- Apply the finish coats flowing the manufacturer's instructions (usually two for best durability).

- Lightly sand in between coats with fine sandpaper and work in a super clean environment for time consuming, but glass smooth results.

284. How to Maintain Timber Indoors

Check regularly any timber in bathrooms or close to external doors, washbasins, showers, washing machines and dishwashers etc for early signs that any surrounding trims are getting damp because of a problem with the finish or indeed from leaks from any of the above appliances etc.

Check for signs of new insect activity, especially in the spring and summer. Look out for small holes and 'frass' (it looks a bit like sawdust). Also, look for any white stains, which could indicate a water leak, especially around any valley (sloping upwards between two different parts of the roof), gully (flat junctions between two roof sections), chimneys or other abutments.

Be especially vigilant looking for evidence of insects if you find any damp timber in your home. Most wood boring insects don't like dry conditions, but they go absolutely gaga for slightly damp timber... it's heaven to them.

285. How to Maintain Timber Outdoors

Protect all exposed timber outside, such as window frames, door frames and timber trims with several coats of paint or other timber preservative such as varnish, timber stain, wax, oil, or other chemical preservative. You should expect to re-apply most types of finishes at set intervals to maintain protection against decay.

Re-application intervals range from a few years in locations exposed to wind and rain or near the coast, to a decade or more in sheltered locations.

Check in the springtime once the weather warms up, look for...

- **Flaking, lifting, or peeling**; caused by several things, poor preparation prior to painting, or just weather and time.

- **Crazing and cracking**, (paint surface looks like alligator or crocodile skin). Could be because of poor preparation prior to painting, mismatched paint types, or an adverse reaction to older paint (i.e. hard oil paint over softer water-based paints), or just too many layers of paint because of extreme old age.

- **Blistering or bubbles**; could be poor preparation again (are you starting to see a pattern with this? Hint, the majority of paint problems are caused by poor preparation... just sayin'), but also trapped moisture or solvent in between coats or even because the paint was applied in the sunshine and the outer layer dried too quick.

- **Chalking**; where aging paint, usually in exposed spots dries to a dusty surface over time.

- **Mildew or mould**; usually in damp areas that don't get a lot of sunshine. Needs cleaning with a cleaner formulated to combat the spores. Spray on with a pump-up garden sprayer and leave to soak and usually rinse off with water. But read the instructions first!

286. How to Maintain Masonry

The absolute best way to protect all types of masonry is to keep it as dry as possible; it's as simple as that. Sounds unlikely I know, it's a wall; but, preventing any wall getting excessively wet will prolong its life considerably.

Minimise unnecessary water from soaking into your masonry by making sure everything is doing its job and there is only one way to do this, yup, you've got to watch it, live, in action... when it's pouring down with rain, the harder the better. No good waiting until it stops, all the interesting stuff is over by then.

Next time it pours down with rain, 'suit up', don your sou'wester or grab an umbrella and go and take a slow walk around your property (ignore the strange looks from the neighbours!) and watch to see where all that water is going, you'll learn lots, or nothing. Both is good; well, one isn't really, as it does mean you have a problem, but looking at it on the bright side, at least you now know what the problem is...

Start at the top and ensure the roof is doing its job and all the water is running off the roof and into the guttering properly and that the gutter isn't overflowing. Check it doesn't dribble back from the roof edge, missing the gutter completely and run down the wall.

Check the amount of 'splash back' (water that bounces up onto the wall from hard paved surfaces). Ideally the ground level is (at least) 150mm (6″) down from your Damp Proof Course (DPC). Make sure any paving at the base of walls drains away from the wall too and doesn't puddle next to the wall. It's a great idea to have a 300mm (12″) loose gravel 'buffer' between any hard paving and the wall (or a small soil border with ground cover type plants) as this also stops rainwater bouncing

up the wall. It still needs to be at least 150mm (6″) down from your DPC though.

Try watching the water running off the capping of any freestanding walls you have when it's raining hard.

Effective cappings (on top) should have a means of stopping the water from running down onto the face of the wall. This is usually a groove cut or cast into the underside of concrete copings (called a drip) or nibs on projecting tiles bedded underneath hard bricks etc.

The drip allows water to fall away from the face of the wall. Ideally, the top part of a wall should have a damp-proof course underneath the capping material as well, but many tradesmen fear that vandals will easily disturb the capping, so it's unusual to find one.

287. Help, my House is all Salty

If you've got white deposits on the wall, often just above ground level and up to about 1m (3′) high. These are soluble salts left behind when water evaporates from a damp wall. Brush them off and carry out further investigation to rectify the cause of the damp.

288. Sealing Moisture in is a Very Bad Idea

A word about sealing your masonry to keep water out. Hmm, some folks love it and others will tell you it'll sound the death knell for your poor wall.

Personally, I think it will end badly if the wall has underlying damp issues. If water is getting into the wall, it must find a way out and if you seal the surface.... yup, it's going to cause damage somewhere as the moisture fights to find a way out.

However, if you've a wall that's rained on whatever you do, or a chimney getting a beating every time it rains, then by all means go for a breathable silicone treatment, with one caveat. Do it at the end of the summer after a long, long period of dry weather to ensure the brickwork is bone dry to start with.

Always follow the instructions as products vary and make sure to find one that's breathable for best results.

289. Is My House Going to Fall Down?

Probably not. But large cracks can be serious if caused by subsidence which is movement associated with damage from nearby large trees or leaking drains etc.

Minor settlement cracking is less serious if caused by the 'normal' settling in of a house over time.

Look out for...

- **Zig zag cracks**: These follow the joints, running across your walls, usually low down. Either 'live' or active and moving; or old and stable. Measure and monitor them over time.

- **Shear cracks**: Straight cracks running up through the bricks and joints; they are always serious. Might indicate a design fault or movement needing attention. Imagine the stress it takes to break fully bedded bricks in mortar. Not good...

- **Large trees**, close to walls: These suck up lots of water drying out the ground, shrinking it. The amount of water varies with the seasons causing the soil to shrink and swell, pushing against the masonry.

  Roots also eventually grow big enough to push against walls and into gaps or cracks where they act like a jack.

- **Tree stumps** close to walls. Large trees take up a lot of water, if removed, the water that once went into the tree causes the soil to swell and 'heave' up, pushing against the masonry.

  I know, the two scenarios, above right? Catch 22 huh! Deciding whether to leave a tree or take it out depends on any evident damage caused, go with the lesser evil...

- **Leaking drains**. Could be leaking for years before anyone notices. A leak washes soil into the drain and away, undermining nearby hardstanding or walls. Look for

sunken areas of garden or paving or leaning or sagging walls.

- **Rainwater systems**. Leaking rainwater systems saturate and destabilise the soil around the base of walls. Make sure your rainwater is going where it's supposed to.

- **Distortion**: Look out for difficulty in opening window or doors. This might indicate wall movement (or old/ poor joinery).

290. How to Look After Render

Some masonry outdoors ends up covered in render (sometimes called stucco). Render is plastering outside basically. This maybe by design from the outset or applied as an attempt to tidy up (read cover-up) a wall in poor condition (with spalled bricks etc.).

Covering poor walls with render rarely works because the source of damp damaging the bricks in the first place, if not rectified, will carry on, eventually blowing the render off the wall as well.

Check render annually. Look out for...

- **Salt**. As with bare masonry, look for wavy lines of white salty marks or deposits on the first metre (3′) from the ground. Often means water is in the wall and evaporating out through the render, leaving the soluble salts behind.

- **Hollow areas**. Gently tap with a piece of wood and listen for odd sounding areas where the render has separated slightly from the wall. Hollow or odd sounding areas are a sign water is behind the render and freezing/ expanding.

- **Bulges and bumps**. Look for actual bulges and bumps which are another sign water is behind the render and freezing (thus swelling and causing the bumps).

- **Edges**. Check the edges, corners, bottom etc. where there might be metal trims going rusty and blowing off the render.

- **DPC**. Look at the bottom edge if it's near the ground, does it cover the damp proof course? Render should NEVER cross the damp proof course as it would allow damp to run straight up the wall.

- **Cracking**. Look for hairline cracks or spalled areas which will be letting in penetrating water, making the wall wet inside. Fill any cracks with outdoor flexible filler and re-paint.

- **Spalling**. Look for spalled, crumbly, or missing areas which are letting in penetrating water, making the wall wet inside.

- **Paint**. Check any paint coverings for integrity and durability.

- **Coverings**. Check any texturing for integrity (Tyrolean, roughcast or pebbledash etc.) Poor quality stuff literally falls off when lightly touched with a paint scraper etc. Replace coating as necessary.

291. Your House Isn't a Garden

As attractive as it can look on certain properties, it's probably best to avoid growing creeping plants up your walls. Although creepers are unlikely to damage the brickwork itself, they can certainly damage doors, windows, guttering and your roof. If you insist on creepers, make sure you cut them back annually at least 300mm (12″) from all the above-mentioned areas, especially at the roofline.

292. Are You Sure You Have Rising Damp?

Genuine rising damp is much less common than you think. Most damp problems stem from using hard cement plasters inside along with poor ventilation and not enough heating. Coupled with rising paving levels outside and cement pointing the brickwork to 'seal it all up'. Some folks go one step further and render the walls to further 'seal' the walls fate.

You can help your old walls massively by restoring them to their original breathable condition...

- No cement-based products inside or out.

- Properly manage the water at the top, i.e. no leaky gutters or downpipes spilling onto the brickwork.

- Make sure the paving level is at least 150mm (6″) below the DPC /floor level.

- Make sure water runs away from the wall.

- Have a soft buffer like gravel or soil/plants next to the wall.

- Don't dry washing inside.

- Use an extract fan or open a window when cooking / ironing etc.

- Have ventilation to ensure a good air flow.

- And if you can afford it, have a decent amount of heating inside to avoid condensation.

I see so many homes where the heating is set to come on for just a short while each day. Essentially this just heats the air in the room; it's not enough to warm the actual fabric of the building.

Mould will grow in all the cold corners where condensation forms. If you're getting any condensation at all; you have a problem of not enough heat and not enough ventilation. Fix it or pay more later.

Do all the above and you might just find that you don't have a rising damp problem after all...

293. Maintaining Your Pipes

Pipes coming into the house don't usually need any maintenance but the pipes going out of the house are another matter.

You'll need to isolate and/or insulate any water pipes exposed to the cold in the winter time (think, outside taps in the garden).

Don't forget the 'other' pipes going out of the house, usually underground. Predictably these pipes carry all sorts of horrible stuff. Sticky stuff, greasy stuff, and stuff they shouldn't be carrying at all, (think plastic, shaving gear, non-bio degradable stuff and even dead pets etc. Oh, and latex stuff, you know what I mean? Yup, don't put those in the toilet either).

Two **totally unbreakable** golden rules. Only stuff you have eaten plus toilet paper in the toilet and never put oils or grease in the sink.

If you put oil and grease down the sink, they will solidify when they hit the cold pipe just outside your house and will build up over time. Always wipe greasy pans with kitchen paper and store used cooking oils responsibly, i.e. in an old 5L plastic container and periodically recycle it.

Google 'fatbergs' to really freak yourself out. Those guys are true heroes, each and every time they go down there.

294. How to Protect Rubber

Try to shield rubber from the worst of the elements. For example, UV rays will damage tyres (especially those not regularly used), turning them grey as the 'carbon black' UV stabiliser gets older and less effective. Seriously consider covering up tyres on stuff you only use occasionally like trailers, motorhomes, RV's, boat trailers, classic cars, and the like, to keep sunshine off the rubber, they'll last longer if you do.

Using your tyres also helps protective waxes built into the tyre; migrate to the surface, protecting them from things like the naturally occurring Ozone in the air, (a great excuse to take out your toys, i.e. "I'm just maintaining the tyres dear; I'll be back in a couple of hours...").

There are various rubber conditioners you can use to top up this built-in protection and slow down deterioration. Spray or wipe the conditioner on tyres, window seals, door seals and weather seals etc.

295. What About Rubber 'O' Rings?

Rubber rings harden over time, cracking or even splitting into several pieces causing dripping or full-blown leaks. Checking and

making sure they are properly lubricated helps maintain a good seal and protects the rubber O ring itself.

Rubber seals called 'O' rings can fail and leak.

They are called 'O' rings because when they leak you'll often hear "O shoot, that seals gone!"

Just kidding, it's because they're round like an 'O'...

To improve an older, neglected O ring, gently remove it and clean with hot, soapy water. Wipe out any old lubricant from the groove it sits in, re-lubricate the seal, and pop it back.

I don't like metal O ring picks (I worry about scratching the groove, causing a leak), preferring instead to use a plastic spudger (no, seriously they are a thing...) or any softer material really, and slide it underneath the ring and to the side to pop up a section, whilst holding the back side to stop it rotating.

Remove bigger external O rings by wiping it dry and 'pinching' it together to lift a section up slightly and then roll it off. The tiniest O rings are difficult to remove without damaging them, so either just wipe them clean and re-lubricate them in situ or replace them with new ones (they are cheap).

Opinions vary on what to use to lubricate O rings, with some controversy around the use of 'PET' or petroleum jelly (Vaseline etc). Most O rings, especially automotive ones are 'petrochemically safe' these days.

Personally, I think PET is better than no lubricant at all 99% of the time, but if you're worried, simply use a dedicated O ring lubricant, especially if you're working on the space shuttle or your deep-sea submersible etc...

296. How to Check Rubber Drivebelts

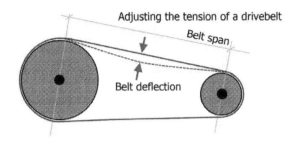

Drive belts stretch and lose tension, resulting in them slipping (listen for squealing usually) and even coming off altogether.

The rubber belt driving engine ancillaries being a classic example. Although often called a 'fan belt' this composite rubber belt rarely drives a cooling fan anymore (most engines have temperature controlled electric fans now), but rubber belts do drive lots of other vital components like power steering, water pump, air conditioning pump (if applicable), and the alternator which provides electrical power.

Most belts are good for the first few years but after this initial period, about once a year check all drive belts for tension and especially look for any micro splits or perishing, especially check the backside on ribbed belts.

As a very rough 'field guide', a drivebelt is correctly tensioned if you can go to the middle of the longest run and twist them through 90° or so (but not much more).

Otherwise, measure the deflection of the belt on its longest run (see the previous image) and compare it to the manufacturer's specifications. There are of course special drive belt tension-measuring tools available if this is going to be a common thing for you.

297. Why Fabrics Wear Out

We mostly wash our clothes to make them smell nice, but washing fabrics also maintains them by removing dust, grit, and dirt. These tiny particles are abrasive and if you add in the friction caused by movement (assuming you don't live on the sofa!), you

have ideal conditions for excess wear and tear.

Fabric worn next to the skin also of course soaks up sweat, which is mildly corrosive to many natural fibres, (yuck a doodle...).

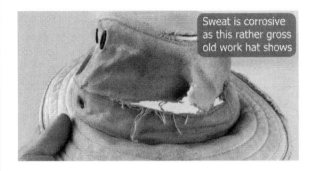
Sweat is corrosive as this rather gross old work hat shows

298. Can You Wash Waterproof Fabrics?

Waterproof fabrics are a little more complicated as there are several different types. Maintenance varies from reapplying an oil or wax to spraying with a water repelling chemical and some you simply wash in a washing machine on a special setting. Read the manufacturers label to find out what type of fabric it is; always follow any aftercare instructions and contact the manufacturer if you can't read the label anymore, as getting this wrong can remove the fabrics waterproofing properties completely.

299. Never Wait to Fix These Things

I general, some things you do on-the-spot as you notice them either indoors, outdoors or on your stuff. Some examples...

- Loose stuff; e.g. a screw in a hinge on a cabinet door.
- Damage to vulnerable coatings; e.g. a stone chip on paint.
- Dry or stiff stuff needing lubrication; e.g. door hinge etc.
- New and unusual sounds need investigating immediately.
- Leaks of any kind, of any liquid, need immediate attention.
- Unusual smells need investigating immediately.

- Unusual vibrations; if it feels different; yup, it needs investigating right away.

300. Painting 101: 34 Professional Tips

I'll end this maintenance section with tips within a tip for a change!

Here's what I've learned watching professional painters for 30 odd years (and no small amount of hands on experience). In no particular order...

1. Buy the most expensive paint brushes for fine work you can find, and then look after them (ordinary brushes are rubbish).

2. Try to work in a clear space. If you can't empty the room (best), then pile everything in the middle (and cover it down) to get at least 1m (3′) of working space, (preferably more) next to the surface to paint.

3. Don't work in awkward positions, and ensure you have good access to the paint, don't overreach or across yourself to get to the paint.

4. Don't even think about painting anything until you have cleaned it thoroughly and allowed enough time for it to dry out.

5. If the finish is solid and just old/faded etc, clean first to remove contaminants and then 'flat' down the surface with fine sandpaper to provide a good key (new paint won't stick to any shiny or glossy surfaces for very long). Sanding also flattens out any old brush marks and highlights any imperfections you might want to fill before continuing, (think, interior woodwork, furniture, crafts etc.).

6. Remember you'll always need to fill holes, nail holes, dents etc. at least twice because filler always shrinks back, leaving dimples.

7. You'll need a very clean working environment when replacing finishes, especially using slow drying oil-based paints and varnishes. This is because any movement causes dust to swirl around and settle onto your wet and sticky project, spoiling the results. Carefully vacuum the whole area and wipe down any horizontal surfaces with a slightly damp cloth before starting. Allow any dampness to dry before applying the finish.

8. Put something on the floor. Seriously, you will drip paint at some point. The minimum is dust sheets/drop cloths, but you'll still need a large square of thick polythene under the actual paint tin, roller tray etc. as anything other than spatter will soak through fabric sheets...

9. Be especially aware not to stand on any paint drips and then tread it all over the new wooden flooring in the next room. Oh, go on then, ask me how I learned that...

10. If you're painting a project on a dusty floor in a garage/shed/etc. and you want a high gloss finish, you should consider putting down polythene or even damping down the floor with a fine spray from a garden sprayer (not so much it splashes when you walk on it).

11. Spray guns (air or airless) are especially good for complex shapes such as staircase spindles or doors with panels etc.

12. Obvious I know, but don't forget to protect any surfaces near where you're working if you're spraying or using aerosols. Paint inevitably seems to drift onto stuff that you don't want painting, (blame Mr Murphy again).

13. Never work from the paint tin. Always 'decant' a smaller amount of paint into a small, manageable size pot, tin, mug, bucket, whatever.

14. When pouring into the above receptacle, always pour from the front side of the paint tin/bucket. Then when the paint drips down the front and you wipe it away with a brush you won't paint over the instructions on the back of the tin (smart huh?).

15. A great painting technique is to apply paint quickly and evenly with a small roller and then immediately go over it with a good quality large brush (called laying off) for a fast, really flat, and professional looking finish on all woodwork.

16. Don't mix tools for paint types. A roller sleeve for water-based paints won't work very well on oil-based paints and vice versa.

17. Seriously consider a very light sanding or flatting in between coats on woodwork projects, it can make all the difference to the smoothness of the final coat. Use a very fine sandpaper (maximum 240grit, preferably finer, say 400grit).

18. Use a roller handle on large rollers, it'll help balance the weight of the roller head when it's full of paint, plus it makes rolling large areas much easier on your poor body.

19. Be aware that you might get a little paint spatter from a roller, especially if you 'roll' too fast. Check horizontal surfaces such as the tops of skirting boards etc., for little paint dots. Slow down, use a finer roller 'nap' or use masking tape to protect areas. Wipe off spatter with a damp cloth as soon as you can.

20. When painting a room, paint trims first, then the ceiling and then the walls... (opinions vary on this though...).

21. Don't stop half way through an area, i.e. keep a wet edge going until you've completed a side/wall etc. Dry edges can be visible after.

22. Be super methodical in your movements with a roller or brush, randomness has no place in painting, paint like a robot would...

23. When dipping a brush in paint, dab the brush against the inside of the paint pot a few times to remove the excess. Don't scrape the brash against the edge of the pot, it removes the paint.

24. If the above tip doesn't work for you and you want to use the rim of the paint tin or bucket to remove the excess (it's a free country), always wipe in the same place to avoid covering the whole rim in paint (keeps the brush handle clean).

25. Practice cutting in to vertical or horizontal corners, glass etc. with a good paintbrush. Masking up takes up a lot of time and isn't always necessary (or very effective, heavy paint easily creeps behind tape).

26. If you do have to use masking tape, make sure you press the inner edge down well (closest to the paint) with a thin flexible scraper (not a finger). The outer edge can be floating, it'll make removal easier.

27. Before removing masking tape off glass, lightly run a sharp blade along its edge to 'cut' the paint.

But really, paint is very easily scraped off glass so learn to cut in without masking off and if you run a little paint onto the glass, don't panic, let it dry and use a blade mounted in a tool to easily scrape it off in seconds.

28. When 'cutting in', don't run a fully loaded paint brush up to the edge, start a little further out and spread the paint along a little first, working down to the very edge with a lightly loaded brush.

29. Don't wash water-based paint out of rollers every day. Wrap it tightly in plastic film to keep the air out.

Wash the roller only when you've finished with that colour. Lasts a few days easily.

30. Before washing a roller sleeve, squeeze the excess paint out of it. Stand the roller on the tray and run a paint scraper down the roller. Turn a little and repeat. A thick pile roller can hold a lot of paint!

31. Don't clean oil-based paint off paintbrushes each day, store them in water (just covering the bristles). Water excludes the air that oil-based paint needs to dry.

Brushes last a long time like this if you remember to check on the water level from time to time.

32. To get the water out of the above brushes before using them again: in a small empty paint tin or bucket, hold the brush between slightly dampened palms, (how you do this is up to you, most folks use a little spit; I know, eww!), rotate the brush between your palms as fast as you can (like a boy scout starting a fire...).

Done properly this flings out any water in the brush. Double check with the old 'brush above the shoulder and a couple of sharp flings down' technique (as if you're throwing a knife into the ground). Best do this outside though...

33. Easily clean water-based paint from your brush at the end of the day using a wire brush (just like combing your hair) and lots of warm water. A pinch of soap doesn't hurt either

34. Lastly and once again (because it's *that* good!), buy the best brushes you can find and look after them. It's a nightmare to get a good finish with cheap (throwaway) brushes and they'll shed bristles too, driving you crazy.

301. Looking After Sharp Edges

A large part of cutting-edge maintenance is not blunting them in the first place by looking after them on the job and storing them in a way that protects their edges.

Don't abuse them by making sure you only use them on the material they were designed for i.e. don't hit nails with a wood chisel.

302. Blow Your Power Tools Out

After just one years use, this jigsaw needs cleaning to remove potentially damaging sawdust.

Power tools benefit from a blow through their air vents with an airline once a year or two. More often if they have been working in a dusty environment, you can buy compressed air in a can if you don't have access to an airline (or take it along to the garage next time you're blowing up a tyre).

303. Power Leads Are Vulnerable

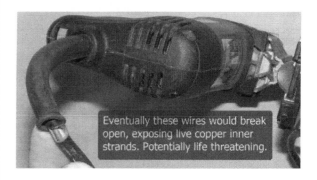
Eventually these wires would break open, exposing live copper inner strands. Potentially life threatening.

Keep an eye on the power leads on your mains operated tools as they fail regularly near the handle. Replace the cable as soon as you see any splits or notice intermittent operation.

REPAIRING STUFF

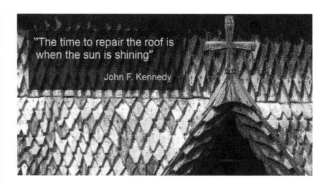
"The time to repair the roof is when the sun is shining"
John F. Kennedy

304. Nothing to Lose and Everything to Gain

If you don't fix it, it's going into landfill. So, there you go, nothing to lose and possibly, everything to gain.

Even if you can't fix it, the experience is great practice and will teach you something small but useful, ready for next time.

305. What the Heck Happened?

Think back in time about exactly what happened, use all your senses and memories... dig deep, it takes time to remember those little signs hovering around the edges of your consciousness.

Think through some of the following...

- Overlooking the obvious happens regularly, (a lot more than you'd think ...). Always check for fuel, power, etc.

- Something changed; (became tight or loose, a new situation, a new or different noise, different circumstances, i.e. it got wet, it dried out, overheated, frozen, etc. etc.)

- Something broke, or came apart, or is missing.

- It started after (insert XYZ event) happened (dropped, got wet, etc.).

- You had noticed a definite problem, but you ignored it, (because you hoped it'd go away, didn't you?).

- It worked fine last time you used it, but now it doesn't.

- It just stopped while you were using it, with no warning.

- It made horrible noises before it stopped.

- It made a specific noise, (bang, groan, knock, pop, scrape, screech, snap, squeal, squawk, tap etc. etc.).

- Something is missing, (a part, a fastener, lubrication etc.).

- It made a funny smell (what did it smell like?)

- Smoke came out of it (which part?).

- It felt funny just before it stopped (vibration etc)

- Something came off (drivebelt, lever etc).

- Now you think about it, there was something odd the last time...

- Or maybe you've had a 'funny feeling' about it for a while.

- It's so tired and worn out, you can't believe it still worked at all...

Is anything on this list ringing any bells for you?

306. Is it Even Worth Fixing?

Before investing any item or money on repairing something, quickly run through these questions in your mind...

- How attached are you to the item, is there any sentimental value?

- How old is the item, roughly?

- What would the normal expected lifespan be? E.g. (laptop = 3 to 4 years, washing machine = 8 years or so, TV = 10 years or so, car = 15 years or so, etc).

- Is it something that's commonly professionally repaired (washing machines for example), or is it an item generally thrown away after failure, such as a toaster or a hair dryer etc.?

- Roughly, what do you think it would cost to get it repaired professionally; is it easy to find out?

- How easy is it to find spare parts to fix it yourself? (Search for the part number or machine serial number online).

- How much will spare parts cost, including shipping etc?

- How long is the spare part delivery time and is there a pressing need to get it fixed quickly? (washing machine being the classic one!)

- How much would it cost to buy a new replacement today?

307. Do You Have the Tools to Fix It?

In addition to the points in tip 300, also think about any tools or equipment you might need...

- Do you have tools to open it up or dismantle it to fit the new parts?

- Do you know anyone who might be willing to lend you the tools? (Friends, neighbours, colleagues etc.).

- If you need to buy new tools, how much do they cost, and will they be useful in the future on other projects? Is the repair worth the investment in new tools?

308. When to Recycle and Get New One

Think about...

- If the repair costs are anywhere close to the cost of a new replacement. Anything even half way needs serious thought.

- Are newer versions more efficient, giving potential money savings in the future? Replacement justification?

- Were you considering an upgrade anyway?

- Sometimes repairs are just not worth it, unless there is love in there somewhere...

309. Some Common Faults, in General

- Sudden stop on electrical stuff could be a tripped breaker or a blown fuse (in the home or in a vehicle).

- Think why though? Unplug or switch off everything and see if the breaker stays on. Switch items on one-by-one and see which item blows the fuse or trips the breaker.

- A sudden or intermittent fault could mean corrosion on a connector and suddenly it has lost its conductivity. Remove connectors and clean with fine sandpaper. Consider protecting the connection to prevent water getting in and corroding it again.

- Intermittent operation or on-and-off operation (when the cable or item moves?) could mean a broken wire in a cable. Replace the cable.

- A sudden stop on an engine could be electrical (might need specialist diagnostic equipment to find item) diagnosis often tricky but repair is usually an easy part replacement.

- A stuttering stop could be fuel related, check any filters, pumps, etc.

- Sluggish operation could mean dirt or corrosion slowing things down. Affects potentially anything that moves; even motors clog up with carbon. Dismantle and clean. Use air and re-lubricate if applicable.

- Things seize solid from either rust or lack of lubrication.

- Snapping, twanging, or rapid slapping noise in a machine could mean a damaged drivebelt. Replace the belt.

- Smoke or bad smells could mean the electrical components burning out or bearings overheating.

- Vibrations from a machine could mean damaged driveshafts or bearings. Replacement is often the only option.

- Grinding noises could mean busted gears or bearings breaking up. Replacement is the only option.

- Linkages can break, bend, or come off their mounting points when retaining clips or mechanisms break.

- Control cables or rods can stretch, snap, or come unsecured at their ends and lose tension.

- Gears can jump, strip their teeth, or rotate freely on their shafts (when the key shears off). Distorted keys are a sure sign of overloading. Keys are usually square or rectangular in cross section but be aware there are such things as offset keys... it's complicated!

- Screws or bolts etc. come undone, strip their threads, or shear off.

- Bearings can break up and fail, (very, very common), sometimes spectacularly.

310. Where Can I Buy Cheap Bearings From?

Never buy new bearings from your machine's manufacturer, because they don't make em! Shocking huh? Making bearings is so specialized, that all machine manufacturers outsource their bearing purchasing from one of the handful of bearing manufacturers worldwide.

This means your bearings are most likely a standard size and you can easily find replacements online (try SimplyBearings.com).

Use a magnifying glass to read the tiny identifying numbers that all bearings carry, usually etched into the outer ring. Make a note of all the numbers and letters you see because each number means something important.

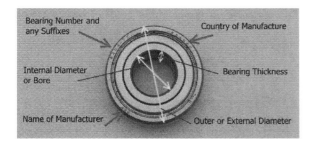

311. Don't Trust Anyone's Story

Remember if someone else used something of yours that subsequently fails, you'll never get the 'full' story. You'll need to tease out the details to find out what exactly happened. Just keep talking; the truth tends to come out gradually, especially if there's any degree of wrongdoing, especially with children, big and small!

Mostly the 'wrongdoing' is through ignorance, and let's be honest here, if you don't own an item, it's not very likely you're very skilled in using said item either, is it?

312. No User Serviceable Parts Inside

What they're really trying to say is "hands off buddy, we'd really prefer it if you go and buy a new one!" But often you can dismantle these parts and at least have a look. Don't worry about 'breaking' it, it's broken already remember.

Oftentimes you'll find single use fixings, such as bend over lugs, plastic welds, glue, or rivets etc. It's often possible to carefully break these open and see if there's anything obviously wrong inside.

Reassembly might require a little creativity though; sometimes you may get away with using the original fold down lugs or tabs.

Other times you need to recreate fixings using glues (superglue, hot glue guns, silicone sealant, general-purpose adhesives etc.) new rivets or... dare I even write it... duct tape and cable ties (I know, I'm a monster) on more agricultural items etc.

Duct tape and cable ties are made in heaven, I kid you not...

Sometimes of course, 'no user serviceable parts' means just that; and you might not be able to do anything useful inside, but by now you should know my theory; i.e. it can't hurt to have a little look now, can it?

313. The First Rule of Opening Something Up

First put something down to protect the work surface (and delicate items,). I like old bed sheets folded up, because stuff doesn't roll around on them (I use old sheets from when the kids were babies).

314. How to Get it Apart by Looking at It

No, young Jedi, not like that! Old school like this. Remember what we looked at earlier, get up close and look for evidence of fasteners. Look for anything that even hints at being a fixing point. Screws are the most obvious, (don't forget to check deep wells or even under labels or rubber feet).

Look for gaps, seams, clips, tiny slots in casting seams or worst of all, nothing (which usually means some sort of adhesive). Not everything is obvious or clear, there may be hidden stuff or multiple types of fixings; in fact, more often than not, this is the case.

Opening glued or welded together stuff is a little destructive. Gently working through the material along the joins or seams with a craft knife, fine toothed wood saw or hacksaw. You could try using a red-hot knife to cut thinner plastic. Hold a thin, sharp blade in the flame of a blowtorch for a minute and then work quickly along the join. Watch the fumes, they'll be dangerous.

On symmetrical casings, round or rotary stuff that could in theory go back together in a different place mark across any joints with a marker pen (or scratch across the join with a sharp implement or even a metal file on heavy or dirty things) before you take it apart. On re-assembly, line up the marks and hey presto, it's back together in exactly the same place.

315. Make Yourself Comfortable

Larger stuff or 'fixed in place stuff' needs some preparation to make working comfortable. Working under the sink on a leaking pipe is much easier if you completely empty the cupboard.

Never struggle on top of loads of junk because you think you'll save a few minutes, you won't. Any kind of crawling around in tight spaces needs good access and if you're underneath something, grab something soft to lay on (no not your significant other). I use an old cot mattress...

It's also a pretty good idea to grab a container or two for putting small parts into as you dismantle. Because I promise you, anything you drop on the floor disappears like magic. Honestly, you'll waste eons of time looking for them, so always use some sort of container. Those ice cream tubs are so useful, aren't they? Yum!

316. It's Easy to Forget Where Stuff Goes

Take a reference photo like this, to ensure everything goes back in exactly the same place.

Make sure you have plenty of room to lay things out logically when dismantling stuff. Ideally mirror the place they came from i.e. working from left to right etc. This really helps to prevent the biggest drag of all time, the 'out of sequence re-assembly'.

Imagine, you get it all back together and yet there is a single bolt left on the bench. Argh! Then you're forced to take it all apart

again, put the bolt where it's supposed to go and then rebuild it all. Tedious, time consuming and worst of all, it'll make you feel stupid.

Really take care during the dismantling phase and the reassembly will go smoothly, I promise. Treat the dismantling phase as 're-verse instructions' to show you how to put it back together again! Plus, you have the old parts to use as a reference for fitting any new parts.

Always take notes and always, always, take lots of photos because they are a great guide and often save the day when you're stuck.

I like refitting each bolt back into its respective hole after removing a part (if possible). This prevents bolts from getting lost or mixed up (esp. good for bolts of differing lengths).

These tips are particularly useful if you're removing something and it will be some time before you'll get back to it because you're waiting for spare parts to arrive or you have other commitments.

317. Going Inside Plastic Cases Can Be Hard

Although plastic casings are usually strong in themselves, they may have little hidden tags and clips that hold some parts together which will easily snap if forced.

Many plastic items consist of plastic mouldings in two halves like a clamshell, simply held together with screws. Remove the screws and the two parts lift apart. Sometimes though, it's screws at one end and then snap fixings or clips at the other end. You might also find clips or lugs that need sliding or turning slightly before lifting away. The screw part is obvious, but if there are clips etc., they might not be.

When separating the casing, knowing where to lever the casing and with how much force to release any clips etc. only comes with trial and error (or bitter experience). Many clips need pushing inwards slightly to release a tiny hook type mechanism.

Start close to where you removed any screws, or if there are slots or indentations. Gently push and pull to see what moves and what is solid. Try carefully inserting a thin blade, (you should seriously consider buying an 'opening tool', they cost pennies) ...

A kitchen knife will do in a pinch, (don't tell the other half and at least wipe it before putting it back the drawer!) into the seam between the parts and lever slightly.

For now, the best advice when separating plastic parts is to go as gently as you can, keep stopping to look really closely, using a magnifying glass and a torch if needed (seriously, it's amazing how useful these are, and not just for old codgers like me). Sometimes you'll get lucky and the clips will spring apart sometimes you won't, (hey, I'm just being honest!).

Never use a screwdriver for levering, unless it's a heavy casing and you can clearly see space for one. Screwdrivers are likely to damage the delicate edges of most casings. Remember, go gently my friend; snapping plastic is a horrible sound...

Once you've removed the fasteners and unclipped the clips and the two parts have initially separated, stop. The side with the fasteners is usually the side you lift away first but be very carefully as you lift it. Keep looking underneath and checking you're not dragging anything out of the lower part, especially wiring, switches, linkages, springs etc.

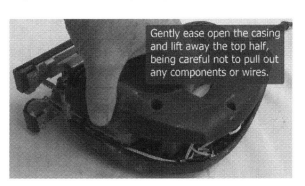

Gently ease open the casing and lift away the top half, being careful not to pull out any components or wires.

318. When Stuff Refuses to Come Apart

Sometimes stuff just does not play nicely, and you need to resort to brute force or be more heavy-handed than you'd like to get stuff apart. The problem is the ignorance part...

If you know how something goes together and it's just stuck (like a car wheel after removing the nuts) then it's safe to use a heavier force.

It's when you're unsure how something fastens together that you can get into trouble, maybe you missed a fixing or maybe there are hidden lugs or catches somewhere and your excess force ends up snapping them.

Sometimes though, you'll reach an impasse and simply can't move forward because the said item simply won't budge. Then you either stop and seek help from a third party or accept there's a risk you might break the item by going forward.

Obviously, this doesn't mean go crazy and yank it apart, you still need to be careful.

Just keep applying force past where you feel comfortable until something gives. Sometimes you'll be lucky, and the item will pop off without damage.

Other times not so much...

319. Logic is Your Reliable Friend

If you're looking at something and it looks scarily complicated... relax, it's fine, it's normal. It'll be all right. Just take a deep breath, remember to go slowly and carefully, and be observant.

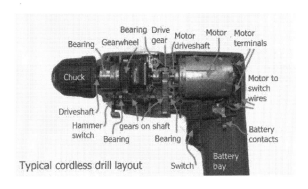

Typical cordless drill layout

This is where you learn what really makes stuff work. Take a look at the inside the above cordless power drill for example...

Take a moment to look at all the parts logically and try to figure out how things move or work inside here. Look at what the various parts are and what they do in relation to each other.

Obviously, the above cordless drill example won't apply if you're working on a wardrobe, but generally, the principle of observation is similar whatever you're looking at. You're trying to follow how stuff operates from start to finish.

It's not necessary to understand the full complexity of what you're looking at, but if you can follow roughly what's supposed to happen, you're more likely to notice anything obviously amiss.

Stuff such as snapped or broken things, missing stuff, things away from their proper location, or stuff that looks out of place or even just something that intuitively feels wrong.

Remember that exploded diagram that you filed away when you bought the item? Now's the time to dig it out or search online for one.

If you can visualise very roughly how something works, this helps you draw conclusions about how it failed.

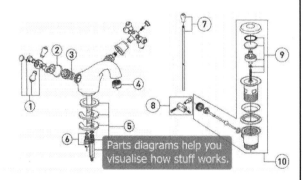

Parts diagrams help you visualise how stuff works.

320. There's Logic in 'Them' Rules

Rules are based on logic and common sense (hopefully). This means stuff like electrical wiring 'should' be in presumed safe zones; i.e. places where it's considered okay for tradesman to place their cables, (search Google images for 'safe zones for electric cables' for more info in your area).

Pipes should also run in logical places according to relevant rules and regulations etc. This means that wires and pipes usually go up or down from outlets and occasionally sideways, but never at an angle (in theory at least...).

In an old house, all bets are off and you might find services in the most unlikely or improbable places, depending on who did the work and when.

Always try to check for hidden cables and pipes, especially before drilling holes in the structure.

Look all around for outlets which obviously point towards wires and pipes etc. and use them to figure out which direction the wires or pipes com into the outlet.

Don't forget that wires etc. can sometimes come into an outlet from the rear, i.e. from the other side of the wall, in another room...

I even found a socket once which was wired from the neighbouring flat and on their electricity bill... (it was in a big house subsequently split into smaller flats).

321. Energy: It's everywhere

Finally, something you learned at school turned out to be useful!

Most machines convert one kind of energy into another; remember those science lessons at school? Some different examples...

- A manual lawnmower converts a push movement into a rotary movement via gears.

- A jigsaw converts the rotary action of a motor into the up and down movement of the blade.

- A heater forces electricity through thin wires causing them to heat up and glow orange, producing heat.

- Electricity illuminates a bulb by forcing itself through wires so thin, that it causes them to become white hot.

- A spring stores movement energy, ready to release when needed.

- A compressor turns the rotary action of a motor driven piston into air stored under pressure via a one-way valve.

- A computer stores up problems, releasing them when it's calculated to be the most inconvenient time for you (joking... maybe?).

322. Always Look for Foreign Bodies

No, not like the CIA. I mean things inside your stuff that's definitely not supposed to be there. Stuff like grit which plays havoc with rubber seals or washers, often causing them to leak. Grit also loves to stick to oils, greases, and other lubrication, making a wonderfully abrasive compound, wearing your stuff out in a flash.

Anything warm or moving attracts dust and other debris. This really builds up over time, especially on fan blades or inside computers etc.

Saw dust and building dust is unavoidable for many electrical tools, as the fan pulls in the airborne dust that's inevitably around.

This fan will work much more efficiently without the sawdust!

In addition, some foreign bodies are an 'inside job', i.e. when something vibrates loose or breaks, falls inside and jams up the works for example. Look for empty holes or broken linkages etc.

323. It's Safe When It's Off, Right?

Err, nope. Lots of common household appliances, such as amplifiers, TV's, some fluorescent tube lamp fittings, microwave ovens, camera flash assemblies, radios, battery chargers etc. have capacitors inside them.

Capacitors hold a charge of electricity to help smooth and stabilise power flows through certain circuits. Some capacitors hold onto this charge for some time. Most small capacitors will drain their power quickly. However, some large capacitors can in theory hold their charge for much longer, sometimes days or even weeks.

Capacitors often look like little batteries, and that's because in a way they are, since they do store up electricity. Also, look for anything with a + or a − sign (positive and negative), as they are a sure indicator that power is around, possibly in the form of a capacitor.

If you want to work on a circuit containing a capacitor, it's best to discharge it first.

You can buy special resistors and tools for this, but most small capacitors will discharge through a small household bulb and a pair of wires. Be careful to not touch anything else to the capacitor terminals or you might get a direct short, a bang, a flash, hot flying debris and smoke (usually in that order!).

I don't recommend directly shorting out a capacitor using a screwdriver, as its unduly cruel to the screwdriver, and the resulting flash/bang will make you jump, and you might hurt yourself...

324. Static Electricity is Harmless, Yes?

Nope again. It might not hurt you that much, but it can definitely kill sensitive electronics.

Get yourself a cheap wrist strap to 'ground' yourself, it's much cheaper than 'losing' a component because of an electrostatic discharge (ESD).

Anything with a circuit board is vulnerable; simply clip the strap to the metal case of the machine or a known 'earth' point.

Damage to components can occur at voltages well below what you can feel (as a crackly spark) and sometimes can it take months before problems manifest themselves.

325. What the Heck is a VoltStick?

A nifty little tool that detects live cables. It also finds breaks in live cables by sliding the tool along until the light goes out, indicating the location of a break. Always check your voltstick is working by touching it to a nearby live point (a switch or power socket front should work).

A cheap voltstick will detect live wires and is your last line of defence to protect yourself against electric shocks.

326. Some Common Problems with Wiring

Wires can cause problems in several ways...

- Overheating (indicating a problem component) causing blackening/burning of the plastic/rubber insulation.

- Wire insulation becomes hard and brittle with age and/or after mild overheating (e.g. putting a 100W bulb into a 40W rated light fitting).

- Loose wires at the connection point, causing arcing, blackening of contacts or intermittent 'on/off' problems.

- A broken wire at a stressed point (repeatedly bent or stretched). A full stop or intermittent on/off problems (e.g. power tool lead).

- Corrosion on connectors if the item has ever been damp.

- Wires occasionally come adrift completely, either the connector itself or the wire out of the connector.

Incidentally, whilst we're talking about wires and overheating. I've seen loads of extension leads melt and two catch fire...

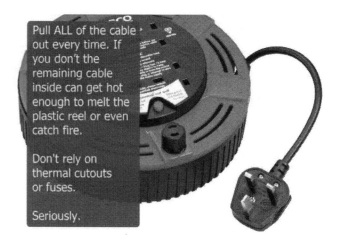

Pull ALL of the cable out every time. If you don't the remaining cable inside can get hot enough to melt the plastic reel or even catch fire.

Don't rely on thermal cutouts or fuses.

Seriously.

327. Always Clamp the Outer Cable

It's common for things to fail because the wires have pulled out of the connectors. Prevent this by always ensuring the outer cable is properly clamped. Small cables might need the clamp turning over to hold properly.

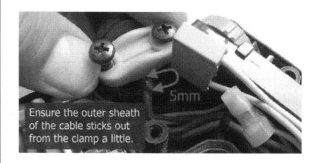

Ensure the outer sheath of the cable sticks out from the clamp a little.

328. Fixing Printed Circuit Boards (PCB's)

Individual failed components on a PCB need special diagnostic equipment (and the knowledge to understand it!) to find. However, that doesn't stop you looking for anything obvious like blackened or melted components. Check online to see if the failed component is available and/ or an 'easy' replacement to fix.

Sometimes the components are fine, but their connections fail when the solder (the silvery stuff melted around the component pins in the board) 'dries out' and cracks, resulting in arcing. Dried out solder joints are a common problem with high load components like control unit PCBs on washing machines.

Look for tiny black sooty deposits or missing solder that looks like 'rings' around component pins. Fix this cheaply by replacing the solder.

Gently wipe the soot away with a cloth and dab the pin with a blob of flux (this chemically cleans the new solder joint). Then touch a hot soldering iron to the pin on one side and hold soldering wire to the other. In a second or two (no longer) the solder will 'run'. Lift off the heat immediately or you'll damage the component.

Never melt solder against the soldering iron tip and allow it to drip onto the surface (the solder will set on the cold surface instantly, without penetrating properly).

Solder must be applied to a cleaned, fluxed and properly heated surface so it can melt and flow without direct contact with the soldering iron. This provides a smooth, even surface, filleting out to a thin edge. For good solder joint strength, parts being soldered must be held in place until the solder solidifies.

Usually though, the quickest and cheapest repair is to replace the whole PCB. Most boards have plug and socket wiring connections, so carefully pinch and wiggle to disconnect or unplug them and remove any screws holding the board in place (after putting on your earth strap or touching an earthed part of the machine's casing).

Gently lift out the old PCB and place the new board in its place and re-affix. Carefully locate the wiring plugs over the sockets on the board and firmly push back in.

329. Original Parts Make Great Templates

If you're replacing something, remember that you already have a good example in front of you. Use it to guide you in fitting the new one.

Offer up the new part to see how it looks using the old part as a reference and of course after reading any instructions supplied, especially exploded parts diagrams. The new part should look the same and turning the part around until it matches the orientation of the original will highlight if there are any differences. Check any numbers stamped or written on both parts. Again, exploded parts diagrams and parts lists will help here...

To replace a part, you must first remove the original. Obvious huh, but it's amazing how many folks don't pay enough attention when removing the original part. Look at everything closely, take photos, make notes etc.

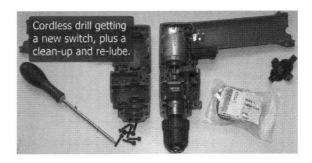

Cordless drill getting a new switch, plus a clean-up and re-lube.

As I mentioned before, it's critical to treat removing the original part as a reverse practice run to show you how to fit the new part, it's the best info you'll ever get.

330. It Still Doesn't Work, WTH?

What can I say? I'm sorry; it happens. Sometimes even with the best of knowledge and intentions, some stuff simply refuses play ball. Sometimes you just can't see why something failed without specialist diagnostic equipment. Or it's one of the increasingly common things with a finite life span.

Console yourself with the fact that some stuff just isn't designed to be fixed. And lastly sometimes stuff is just plain worn out and realistically, you never had a chance from the start.

However, Auguste Rodin once said, 'Nothing is a waste of time if you use the experience wisely'. Make failure motivate, not discourage you, because you've gained valuable dismantling experience, plus you now understand a little more about how that particular thing works.

331. Just Chuck it in the Bin Then?

Not yet. Remove and recover any potentially useful things. Cables and plugs, fittings like brackets, handles, hinges, wheels, nuts and bolts or other fasteners. It's even worth saving any usable metal, plastic, or other materials. Fill up your 'bits and bobs' drawer with invaluable stuff to be useful on another repairs and projects.

332. Hot Glue for Temporarily Holds

Hot glue is great to temporarily hold stuff, because it doesn't penetrate. It's ideal for stuff too small for regular clamps or awkwardly placed stuff. Tap to remove and residue cleans off easily. Place quickly though, it starts to set like lightning!

333. Don't Have a Clamp? No Problem

Make your own powerful tourniquet clamps using some cord and a stick.

Simply tie the cord around and thread the stick through and wind it up, wedging the stick once tight (sometimes called a 'Spanish windlass').

You can make your own with a piece of cord and a stick, (or elastic bands or even just tape pulled tight for small stuff).

Just remember these are powerful and can easily be tightened enough to break stuff.

334. Timber Dings, Dents & Scratches

If timber is bare or oiled, you can often lift out shallow dents by placing a drop of water in the dent. Then pop a damp cloth over the damage and firmly rub a hot iron over the damage.

Wait a minute in between rubs to give the fibres time to swell. Repeat as necessary.

The hot steam swells the fibres, lifting them up. This method is also worth a try on shallow scratches too, it won't hide any cut fibres, but it will lift any compressed ones making the damage smaller and therefore a little less visible.

335. Magic Wax Repair Sticks

Wax type sticks are perfect for hiding scratches and small imperfections etc. in timber surfaces. There are various colours (even white to repair dings in melamine/cabinets etc.), and you might need to mix two together to get the exact match.

Simply work the warmed coloured wax into the mark and scrape off any excess with a flat blade. A rag dipped in a spirit will tidy up the edges if it smeared a little.

I've even seen children's wax crayons and even shoe polish used to good effect, hiding small imperfections, ideal for after those 'parents are away parties' (whistles innocently...).

336. Repairing Old Walls: One Rule

Generally, walls built between the fifteenth century and the Second World War walls (in the UK at least) used a lime-based mortar (softer mortar, easily scraped out with a screwdriver or even a fingernail) and are usually solid (i.e. one brick thick/ two half bricks thick, (or more on larger structures), with no air gap or cavity).

We touched on this before under maintenance, but it bears repeating; never, ever use a cement-based mortar to repair a wall built using lime-mortar, because it forces moisture inside the wall to evaporate from the brick itself, which then freezes etc. often causing spalling of the brick face, especially the edges...

Always use lime products to repair walls built with lime mortar.

337. My Mortar Joints Have Eroded, Panic?

Not just yet. Lime mortar joints are sacrificial by design, i.e. any moisture trapped in the wall should evaporate from the joint, eroding it gently over the millennia. So don't panic if your mortar joints are eroding, they're supposed to. It's much better for the wall for moisture to evaporate from the joints, as this protects the bricks which are much more difficult to replace or repair.

Generally, re-pointing your mortar joints in a matching mortar can wait until the joints have eroded at least 13mm (1/2″) and not a moment before; the only exception being if a particularly exposed wall is letting water penetrate through to the inside, causing damp issues.

338. Lime Mortar is Complicated Isn't it?

No. Re-pointing using lime mortar is a perfect DIY proposition, despite the fear lime mortar evokes amongst even professional tradesman. Working slow and carefully suits lime mortar (due to its long setting time) making it a perfect project for you.

There's plenty of free advice about lime mortar out there, much of it from local authorities or conservation organisations. If you have a specific query, you can call the very helpful guys at SPAB (Society for the Protection of Ancient Buildings) in the UK, who are all heroes regarding lime mortar, they are probably all devilishly handsome too, so give them a call...

339. How to Chop Out a Spalled Brick

Using a club hammer and cold chisel or small bolster chisel always ensure you're chopping in towards the middle of the brick.

Never, and I mean never, lever (or even touch) the chisel against the edges of the surrounding bricks to try and lever a piece out, you will chip them... 100% guaranteed.

We've all done it, don't worry, so go ahead, you'll learn one way or another just how 'chippable' bricks are!

Some folks hit the brick directly with the hammer a few times to 'break it up', this does work, if you're an accurate shot and sure you're going to hit the right brick...

340. Will My House Fall Down?

It's possible. But generally, if you're repairing a small area of spalled bricks, up to one metre wide, the brickwork is self-supporting (like the next image). But if there are additional factors, such as a corner or you're underneath a window etc. add additional support using adjustable steel props etc. for the duration of the repair.

Damage removed, cleaned out and ready for damping down prior to re-building.

One very important last thing; ensure the last or top joint is completely full of mortar. Yes, I know it's difficult and time consuming to push little bits of mortar all the way to the back and pack the joint solidly, but really, if you don't, the replaced bricks will not hold the weight above, quite literally...

Use a finger trowel slightly thinner than the joint (I custom make my own by cutting down cheap pointing trowels), push the mortar onto the top of the brick and then to the right, packing it tight, all the way to the back, repeat until the whole joint is full.

341. How to Replace a Concrete Roof Tile?

Replace a concrete tile (or plain tile), by pushing the row above up a little until it clears the top of your chosen tile. If the tiles above are nailed though, lift them up as far as they will go and use door stops or wooden wedges to hold them up.

Wiggle out any broken pieces of the old tile and pop the new one in. Pull down the row above or remove the wedges.

Jiggle (technical term!) all the tiles around the new one to ensure everything seats properly and lays flat. You'll need a small trowel to lift up the tiles enough to get your fingers underneath. A pair of gloves is handy unless you've hands like a gorilla and don't need to worry about snagging anyone's stockings...

342. Never Use Steel Nails for Roofing Tiles

Because they are too hard. In general, use softer aluminium nails for fastening roof tiles to avoid cracking the tile on the last couple of hits. It's traditional to use copper nails for slate though. You don't need to hammer them in really tight (you'll still risk cracking the tile, leading it to fail after a short time), just lightly up to the tile is usually sufficient.

343. Do my Ridge Tiles Need Re-pointing?

No, hardly ever. There is little point in 'pointing up' over old mortar, if you can lift the ridge tile off by hand, do so, clean it up and re-bed it in fresh, stiff-ish mortar mix consisting of 1:1:2, cement/grit or sharp sand/soft sand. Place broken bits of tile underneath any larger gaps (in between ridge tiles etc.) to support the mortar.

If you can't pull the tile off by hand, then leave them alone (check them again next year) and go fishing instead.

The modern trend is heading towards dry fixing methods (nails, clips, and wires) so expect to see mortar disappear for good on roofs in the very near future.

344. How to Easily Point Paving

Without getting mortar all over the paving surface. Cut a square of thick polythene (or linoleum) 300mm or 12″ square and cut a slit in it about 200mm or 8″ long. Position the cut over the joint and drop the mortar through it and into the joint between the paving (you can do this quite hard to get the mortar deep into the gap) . Scrape off excess mortar, move the guide along and repeat. Go back occasionally and finish off the joint surface as you wish.

345. What to do if a Pipe Freezes

Frozen pipes will split open when they thaw (or occasionally it will just push open the fittings). Cut damaged sections out with a rotary pipe cutter and insert new sections and pairs of new fittings, compression, or plastic push fit usually. You can replace any soldered fittings with push on ones as above.

Making room to get new fitting in means finding some wiggle room to get the ends of the pipes into the fitting. Unclip what you can to create some slack or carefully bend the pipes outward (or up or down) just enough to get the fittings on (mark the pipes so you know they are in far enough). Double check everything is fully home and tight before switching on the water (it's easy to forget to tighten up something).

Fit an isolation valve into the new repair if possible then you can switch it off next year. Insulate what you can up to the valve to prevent a repeat occurrence.

346. Finding Leaks in Underground Pipes

To find damaged underground drain pipes look closely at the ground along any drain runs, (from grates to access points and in between access points for example) because when drains leak, often material surrounding the pipe washes away down the drains.

This erosion eventually causes depressions in the ground or subsidence under walls and hard standing areas etc., clear giveaways there's a problem below the surface.

Oh, and leaking drains always leads to...

Roots, because they just love leaking drains and will seek them out like crazy. Wrapping themselves around and into any gaps or cracks like an octopus.

All those lovely nutrients flowing right on by make for happy plants... Left long enough they'll fill the pipe.

Roots of all kinds just love leaking drains, it's all those juicy nutrients...

Alternatively, hire a drain camera to see exactly what is going on underground. Cameras are locatable from the surface, so you always know exactly where they are, (handy if you see any damage via the camera).

If the damage is deep underground or in an inaccessible location, consider hiring in a specialist who may be able to insert a sleeve and repair the drain from inside, without digging it up. Not a cheap prospect, but probably much cheaper than a complete dig up.

It's possible to make a homemade drain camera using a cheap USB endoscope camera fastened to a set of drain rods and a laptop (tape the camera in the middle of the screw attachment).

I once cable tied my kids old waterproof video camera onto an old roller-skate once. Then I used my drain rods connected to the roller-skate to push the camera down an 200mm (8") surface water drain at my place to find a problem.

Recorded about 20m (65') of footage and watched it back on the laptop. Worked brilliantly and found the problem.

347. How to Repair a Broken Drain Pipe

Cut the broken section out and discard (tool depends on the material). Push two lubricated slip collars or rubber pipe connectors all the way onto the cut ends. Measure the gap in between the new slip collars and cut a piece of new pipe to fit tightly into the gap.

Chamfer the cut ends and smear pipe lubricant onto the pipe ends. Wiggle the new pipe into the gap. Push, rotate and slide each slip collar/joint onto the new section of pipe until the new collar/joint is half way over each joint. It helps if you mark the pipe about 60mm (2 ½") back from the ends, then you'll know when you've centred the slip collars.

Surround the repaired pipe preferably with pea gravel, or in a pinch with the soft 'as dug out' material. Once the pipe's covered, backfill the hole to the top, compacting as you go with your boots, leaving it a little high as the 'backfill' will settle a little in time.

348. Can I Nail Up My New Drywall?

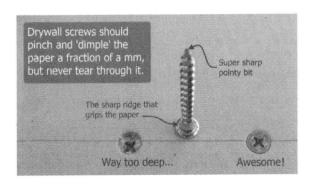
Drywall screws should pinch and 'dimple' the paper a fraction of a mm, but never tear through it.
Super sharp pointy bit
The sharp ridge that grips the paper
Way too deep...
Awesome!

Nails are defunct nowadays for fastening up drywall, so use drywalls screws as they hold much better. The most important skill to learn when installing drywall is... knowing when to stop driving in your screws!

349. How Can I Put Up Drywall on my Own?

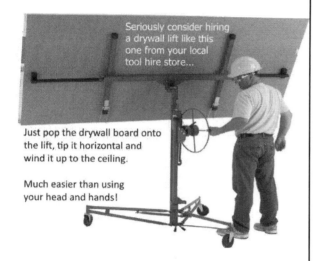

Seriously consider hiring a drywall lift like this one from your local tool hire store...

Just pop the drywall board onto the lift, tip it horizontal and wind it up to the ceiling.

Much easier than using your head and hands!

Working overhead with heavy boards is difficult. i.e. balancing the board on top of your head whilst you grab the drill driver from in between your knees to drive in the first screw. Without the board moving. Not easy.

You should be able to hire a simple drywall lift at your local tool hire store. They are brilliant and you'll make a much better job using one as you can use bigger boards and position them easily.

If you don't have the possibility to hire a drywall lift, make up a couple of 'dead men' from some scrap timber. These dead men are like a third hand and will help hold up a board whilst you get a screw in.

Make them about 12mm (½″) taller than the height between the floor and finished ceiling height so that they just 'wedge' in place.

350. How to Repair a Small Hole in Drywall

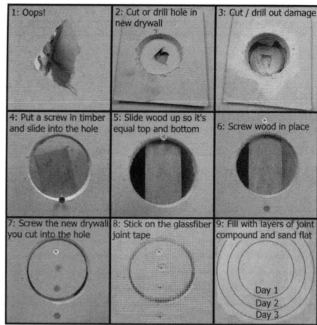

351. I'm *Not* Asking for a ButtBoard...

There are a few different ways of managing the awkward 'short side' joints in drywall centred around this rather awkwardly named technique...

The short sides of tapered edge drywall boards have no taper (don't ask me why!).

An easy way to overcome this, is to let the joint in between two drywall boards 'float' in the gap between studs and use one of these 'flying butt joint' methods.

You can make butt joints several different ways.

- Use a proprietary butt joint system (see next image).

- Add extra timber noggins recessed 3mm into the area behind the board joints.

- Make your own back-block "butt boards' out of 150mm strips of plywood or OSB (Oriented strand board) with 3mm (⅛″) packing strips at the edges.

- Or run the same Plywood or OSB strips through a table saw twice, to create a very shallow 2-3mm (⅛″) depression in the middle of the board.

You tape and fill recessed butt joints exactly the same way as you do the long-tapered sides which saves time and material. Here is the propriety Buttboard system from Trim-Tex ...

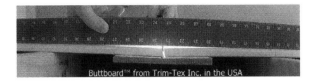

Buttboard™ from Trim-Tex Inc. in the USA

Or you can make your own...

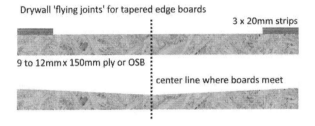

Drywall 'flying joints' for tapered edge boards

3 x 20mm strips

9 to 12mm x 150mm ply or OSB

center line where boards meet

Incidentally, the traditional way is to fix the ends of the drywall over a stud and tape over the flush joints and then 'feather' out joint compound either side of the joint. Takes several layers and takes skill to do well without leaving a visible bump.

352. It's Always Sharp on the Backside

Cutting metal always produces a burr on the back side of the cut. Easily 'de-burr' them by running a file across them at an angle.

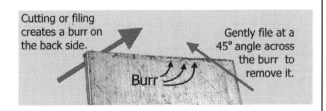

Cutting or filing creates a burr on the back side.

Gently file at a 45° angle across the burr to remove it.

Burr

353. I Fixed it, But Oh...

Don't fix one problem and cause another. Men are particularly good at this; i.e. when they are so focused on the job in hand, they're plonking tools down on unprotected worktops or tables etc.

Protect vulnerable surfaces by making some 600mm × 900mm (2′ × 3′) surface protectors out of carpet offcuts; then you can put your tools down knowing you're not going to damage anything.

A friend of mine gets his by asking at the local carpet store for old sample pieces. These lovely felt backed 600mm (2′) squares with bound edges spread out on work surfaces really emphasises his care and professionalism.

354. I Put it Down and Now I Can't Pick it Up

Never put anything really heavy straight on the floor because you'll have a devil of a job to pick it up again. Always put a few pieces of old timber on the floor first and put anything heavy on the timber. That way you have a gap underneath which makes picking it up a whole lot easier.

Fork lift truck drivers do this all the time obviously, otherwise they would never get their forks underneath the object, be like a fork lift truck driver...

355. Concrete is Really Hard to Remove

Er, duh! Concrete is predictably pretty hard stuff, so it's no great surprise that it's tough to remove. But there are some tricks you can use to make the job easier.

First, enrol at your local gym and hit the weights. Second (only kidding). Nope, muscles will help you, but technique; now there's a heavy hitter.

You see, concrete is incredibly strong (bear with me) ... but only in compression. In tension, not so much. The secret is to attack the concrete at its weakest point and that's at any corners or edges, where it's in tension and not supported very well.

Hitting it at the edge applies the force across the slab, putting the top in tension. You're not trying to crush it (where it's strong), you're trying to snap it, (where it's weak).

If you can lever the slab up a little using a large bar, (even a tiny bit) you'll create lots more tension in the slab and find it even easier! Hitting concrete in the middle will never break it., i.e. because it's surrounded (and supported) on all sides by more concrete. The hammer will just bounce off (and that hurts a bit actually).

356. No Shorts When Removing Concrete

A word about shrapnel (and no, you don't need to head for your bunker!). You're applying huge forces when you hit concrete with a sledgehammer and part of the surface shatters into lots of small pieces, some of which will fly out in all directions.

So, save your shorts for the beer after you've finished and wear sturdy trousers for this job. Oh, and don't forget to prop sheets of plywood up against anything breakable. You know, like doors and windows. Don't say I didn't warn you...

357. Use a Wrecking Bar on Concrete

Once you've broken a piece of concrete and have a good-sized crack, try a long pry bar to lever away sections of concrete. Pry bars work amazingly well because the remaining slab is a very good point to lever against as it's immovable. Using bars like this applies a huge force against the little piece you're trying to shift, to great effect.

358. Never Let Grinder Sparks Hit Glass

Because they can be hot enough to embed themselves. I once ruined the rear windscreen on my old Daimler cutting rusty metal out of the floor, lesson learned the hard way.

359. How to Find Fasteners Behind Drywall

You can of course buy a special detector but much cheaper are magnets. Wrap a small, powerful earth magnet in tissue or thin cloth, suspended from a string, hold the string and magnet on the wall, moving it back and forth where you suspect there are screws/nails (you'll feel a 'pull' as it passes any metal).

On true drywall (not skimmed /veneered plastered) you might see the tiny depressions over the fasteners (because most fillers shrink slightly) by shining a torch across the painted surface. Logically, finding the fasteners tells you where the timber studs are...

360. How to Remove Drywall Fasteners

After finding them as above. Use a pointed bradawl or similar, to pick out the plaster or filler over the fasteners and then remove them with a screwdriver. Once the fasteners are out, lever out a board edge and pull out the drywall, joint tape breaks easily.

361. Sawing a Vertical Stud Out of a Wall

Never saw through a timber stud squarely, it will jam and pinch the saw blade. Always saw through the stud downwards at an angle. This method works well when removing window and door frames too.

362. Hacksaws Are Rubbish for Pipes

Never put a pipe you've sawn off with a hacksaw into a push-fit fitting because the burs around the end are too rough. Always use a rotary pipe cutter which leaves neat, slightly rounded pipe ends which won't damage the O rings inside the fittings.

MAKING STUFF FROM SCRATCH

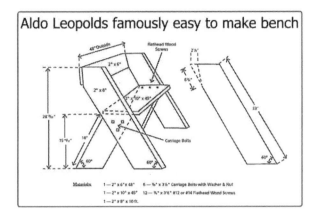

363. Aldo Leopold's Iconic Bench

How about Aldo Leopold's famously easy to make bench pictured above? The simple joinery is perfect for beginners, with only straight cuts and mechanical joints.

Plus, it'll look great in the garden as well as being a perfect place to read instructions or for a well-earned coffee break.

364. Or Even a Small Boat?

About as much fun as you can have with 'one and half sheets' of plywood, ideal for small and big kids alike.

Me and my son built a little plywood 'mouse' boat using freely available plans from the internet and Gavin Atkins book '17 plywood boats anyone can build.'. So simple, so cheap, and so, so much fun! Talk about a conversation starter when it's on the roof rack!

365. Make a Door Holder

This simple door holder makes taking a little off the side of a door easy. Take a short piece of 50mm × 100mm (2″ × 4″) timber, around 60 to 90cm (2′ to 3') long and cut a 35mm deep slot through it, just wider than a door.

Lay the door into the slot and secure it with a long, tapered wedge (cut from the side of the timber), it works even better if you match the angle of the wedge on one side of the slot.

366. Borrow Designs from Others

The more artistic amongst you might want to design your own stuff. But for everyone else, take a look at the many plans available online, both free and paid for. Although step-by-step instructions leave little to the imagination, they are a great starting point for you if you're a new in the handy game. Following a properly designed set of plans takes the guess work out of a project, especially if the plan supplier has an active support system like a forum where you can ask for help from others who are in the same boat (well, not literally; unless you're actually building a boat of course...).

Working to a well-produced and detailed plan also gives you the confidence to try new techniques or tools for the first time, because you know the end result will fit and is a good design.

Working to plans might even allow you to tackle a project above your perceived skill level. For example, the vast majority of boat plans sell to people who have never built a boat before, although I'd recommend you aim more towards the bird box end of the scale to start off with, until you have a little more experience with your tools.

Who knows, you might even write your own one-day, because when you look through some of the books in the library, you might think, 'I could do better than that.'

367. Some Thoughts About Setting Out Tiles

Symmetry and balance are important in nearly all cases. When tiling a wall, you can't just start at one end and work left to right, it will look terrible, seriously, (unless you're very lucky with the spacing).

When tiling a wall, measure or preferably set out dry tiles along each wall (or on the floor) starting in the middle of the wall and working out to the edges. If you end up with a small cut at the end, go back and start with a full tile in the middle instead and set out again to get a bigger cut at the edges.

All tiling looks best if you avoid small pieces of tile, because they are difficult to cut. Sometimes you can 'roll' larger tile offcuts around the corner and carry on which looks good, but not if there is something else on the new wall which needs centring (see next paragraph). I know, it sounds complicated and that's because it is complicated; that's why you see terribly finished tiling everywhere...

Alternatively, if there is something on the wall, it's best to start in the middle of it, so the cuts are the same size each side (think windows, doors, kitchen hob extractors, sinks, bathroom basins, toilets etc.).

If there are several things on the same wall, such as a window and a door or a basin and a toilet, you've got some serious juggling to do to get it to look right. Choose the window usually or try centring the material at different points and chose the one which looks best to the eye.

Never, and again I really do mean never, fix the first tile unless you know exactly where the last tile is going.

368. Someone Has Thought This Through

Almost everything in construction is modular. By this, I mean that material sizes and spacing measurements are rarely random but designed to fit somewhere specific. For example...

- Two bricks side by side are the same length as one brick lengthways plus room for a joint, ideal for half bond walling...

- If you set out timber studs at 400mm or 600mm (16″ or 24″) centre-to-centre, then 2400mm × 1200mm (8′x4′) drywall sheets will fit perfectly.

- If you set out floor joists at 600mm centre-to-centre, then 2400mm × 600mm chipboard flooring sheets fit perfectly. Although if you're gluing the joints (and you should be) then 'flying joints' are cool.

- Builders metalwork like joist hangers etc. will fit standard 47mm (2″) timbers (smaller and larger sizes are also available).

- Kitchen units come in a range of sizes based on 100mm (4″) so you'll see units in multiples of 100mm. i.e. 300, 400, 500, 600, 800, 1000mm etc. to name a few common ones.

- 600mm (24″) white goods such as dishwashers, washing machines and fridges etc. will fit into an exact 600mm (24″) gap between kitchen units (because all white goods are slightly undersized).

- Timber sizes run around 25mm (1″) or multiples thereof. So, you'll see timber 25, 50, 75, 100mm thick and the same in height, 25, 50, 75, 100, 125, 150, 175, 200, 225mm etc.

- Timber lengths run around 300mm (12″) units, so you'll commonly see 2400mm, 2700mm, 3000mm, 3300mm, 3600mm, 3900mm, 4200mm, 4500mm, 4800mm and sometimes 5100mm or more (8′, 9′, 10′, 11′, 12′, 13′, 14′, 15′, 16′, 17′ etc.).

369. When is 50mm not 50mm?

A small aside at this point. Re tip 369, actually most timber is slightly undersized to allow for regularising (extra machining to make the timber a consistent size), so 50mm is more likely to actually measure 47mm and a

200mm deep floor joist might only actually be 195mm etc.

370. How to Avoid Modular Mishaps

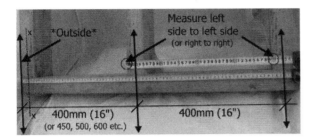

One thing to remember about modular stuff is that you need to make allowances for the first spacing. Using one of the above examples, if you set out a timber stud wall with the studs at 400mm centres, when you offer up your first drywall board, you'll find you're a little short because you set out or started your spacing from the centre of the first stud and not the outside of the new wall.

Always set the centre of the second stud 400mm (etc.) from the wall and not the middle of the first stud next to the wall.

Always keep any odd spacing's to the edges or you'll end up cutting boards to fit in the middle of the wall which is inefficient.

Always accurately set out stuff like first floor joists, ceiling joists, and studwork for example, to make it easy to fit subsequent materials such as drywall or floor boards.

371. X Really Does Mark the Spot

Always indicate with a cross, which side of your mark the item is to go!

372. Centre to Centre is Flexible

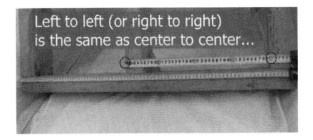

Working to centres is largely a figure of speech because although in theory, you're setting out centre-to-centre; in practice, it's difficult to measure from the middle of one thing to the middle of another.

More likely you'll be measuring from the outside-to-outside or inside-to-inside, which when you think about it, is actually the same thing, as long as you start the first one in the right place.

373. So Many Tools for Cutting Timber

The tool to use is dependent on the size and length of the timber. Use the tips below to decide how best to cut your timber and with what tool...

- A regular handsaw is fine for just about anything if you don't mind sweating a little! Gentle curves are possible too.

- Jigsaws are fair for straight cuts through thin material, good for rough (ish) square cuts and great for curves in flat panels etc.

- Hand held circular saws are good for straight cross or rip cuts in timber and panels. Be careful crosscutting smaller timbers as the blade can snatch dangerously (support the workpiece well).

- Cross cut or mitre saws are good for general cross cutting to length and of course mitre cuts.

- Table saws are great for resizing timber stock and panels.

- Plunge saws are good for panel work and cutting out square holes etc. Quick and easy to set up with great cut quality (minimal splintering due to the fine, multi toothed blade).

- Flip over saws combine a table saw and a mitre saw, making them a very versatile tool (it's my personal weapon of choice!).

374. Each Piece of Timber is Different

Timber is obviously not a 'man made' product and as such, each piece is different. You'll need to check each piece to ensure its suitability for the job in hand.

Check for defects, check for differing grain patterns or colours (if placing together with other pieces). Keep grain and colour disruption to a minimum if you can. There is often a large variation in colour, this might look odd in certain situations (a pair of doors for example).

Keep poor pieces to one side for that moment when you need a short length, or a piece that will not be so readily seen etc.

375. Jigsaws Are Brilliant... and Hopeless

Jigsaws are great for cutting curves in plywood, cutting roofing timbers, not so much. Realise their limitations.

Jigsaw blades are thin and wander quite badly generally, so only use very sharp blades and change them regularly. Look for thicker blades with a 'square cut' icon on them, being made from thicker metal, they cut square.

376. You Need all the Support You Can Get

When cutting timber, you need to support the workpiece properly. Most cutting problems arise from inadequate support, i.e. the timber moves and pinches the blade with unpredictable consequences.

I seriously recommend you invest in a foldable workbench or some trestles to support your workpiece whilst working on it, oh and a 'quick clamp' or two is a good idea too to securely hold the workpiece down.

Good support is especially important during those last few milliseconds of sawing to prevent pieces falling onto the floor and tearing away the corner.

Trestles or old-fashioned sawhorses and two or three planks (scaffold boards, or lengths of stout timber) make a great impromptu workbench.

377. Plunge Saws Will Take Over the World

Because they are just that good. If funds allow, treat yourself to a good pro. quality plunge saw as these are brilliant for beginners and professionals alike.

They are pretty infallible because the saw sits and rides along a guide. Admittedly, they are not cheap and are quite sophisticated, but boy are they great for cutting sheet materials or even holes out of worktops etc.

Simply mark where you want the cut, place the rubber edge of the guide on the pencil mark, set the depth of cut and lower the saw into the workpiece, gently slide along, release and lift. No measuring back from a line to allow for the size of the saw etc., because it cuts exactly on the rubber guide edge. Exactly.

They are fast, easy to use and leave a superior finished cut because of the fine multi-toothed blade.

378. If You Ever Stop a Power Saw Mid Cut

If you need to stop any power saw for any reason, always pull the workpiece away from the blade, or pull the saw back a little. This stops blades teeth snatching the wood and jumping all over when you start up again.

379. it Matters Which Way the Grain Runs

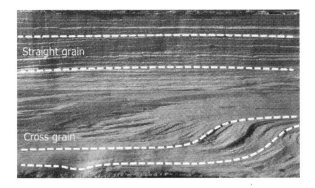

When it comes to removing wood and shaping it with a plane or a chisel etc, you need to look at the way the grain runs to avoid your tools 'tearing out'.

Picture wood grain being like a handful of fibres roughly going the same direction, like a handful of straw.

You must always be cutting down or with and across the fibres (grain), never up into or against them, otherwise the grain will 'tear' out bits of timber leaving an unsightly finish.

Experiment on scrap off-cuts first to get a feel of when the timber 'tears' and how it behaves under a plane or a chisel.

Again, make sure the workpiece is secure, as pushing a plane exerts considerable force. Nail a thin 'stop' timber to the workbench and push the workpiece up to it; this will stop the workpiece sliding down the bench as you plane. Use a regular quick clamp if you're using a chisel etc.

Adjust the plane until it's taking little more than a whisper of timber away, if it digs in, you're trying to cut too deep or going into the grain. Think about the relationship between how much you are removing and how hard it is to push. Sometimes less really is more, because it's much easier and quicker to remove lots and lots of thin layers instead of pushing hard to remove a thicker layer, plus you'll get a finer finish. A properly sharp plane

blade will leave a surface finish which needs little sanding.

Most often you'll find it easier to push the blade at a slight angle across the grain too. Hold the tool at a slight angle across the workpiece and push it straight down the timber following the grain.

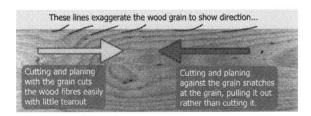

Hardness and grain direction vary from species to species and this affects the timbers 'workability'. Very hard timbers like seasoned oak or timber known for its gnarly grain like maple etc., require razor sharp edges on your tools and a good understanding of grain direction for success. Fortunately, the most commonly available 'white' timber you'll see in the store are some of the easiest to work with as they are soft and have relatively straight grain.

380. How to Use a Plane on End Grain

Plane blades will break off a big lump of timber as it grabs the last bit of wood when planing across end grain.

There are lots of ways to prevent this though, (first, make sure the blade is extremely sharp); but the three simplest ones are as follows...

- Fig 1: Plane from each end towards the middle. Because the grain will tear up a little on the 'wrong' side, in practice this means you should plane mostly along the grain and then turn around near then end so that you're only planing against the grain for a short distance.

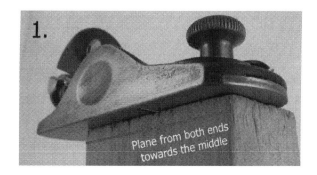

Plane from both ends towards the middle

- Fig 2: Plane a small 45° chamfer across the end of the workpiece and plane straight over it. Keep checking it's still there as it will reduce in size as you plane the end down, you might need to re-plane a new angle if you are taking a lot of material off the end of the workpiece.

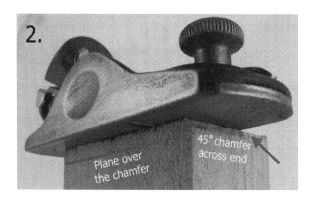

Plane over the chamfer

45° chamfer across end

- Fig 3: Clamp some scrap wood on the backside of the workpiece to act as a sacrificial piece (i.e. where it doesn't matter if it chips a little).

Plane over a piece of scrap wood clamped to the end

381. Quick and Dirty Guide to Sandpaper

Finish stuff off using sandpaper for a really nice surface, either by hand or on a machine. Detail or part sheet sanders use a flat, vibrating plate to remove material but a belt sander will remove large amounts of material.

40, 60 and 80 grits are aggressive for initial sanding with 120, 150 and 180 giving a smooth finish. 240 and up is for furniture work mostly and give a spectacularly fine finish.

Personally, for most domestic construction use I get by with 40 grit for removing rough stuff and 120 grit for finishing up anything ready for the decorator, but then I am a hairy old builder and any cabinet makers reading this will have a heart attack at this recommendation...

Basically, start coarse and gradually use finer and finer sandpaper (and yes, it takes ages...), oh, and don't forget your dust mask.

If your sandpaper gets clogged. Use a wire brush to unclog it.

382. Some Notes About Sheet Materials

- **Chipboard** (particle board). Essentially wood chips and glue, compressed in to a hard and rigid board perfect for flooring and furniture making.

- **Melamine** faced chipboard (laminated melamine particle board). Ideal for cabinets and furniture making. Mainly white but available in various colours.

- **Plywood**. Multiple thin veneers of real wood glued together in alternating grain directions to produce a hugely strong composite board. With a range of different face finishes, from melamine laminates to real-wood veneers such as oak, teak, birch, beech etc.

- **Exterior grade plywood**. As above but with weather proof glues (in reality, pretty poor if they get wet though).

- **Marine plywood**. As above but with waterproof glues (okay to get wet, but the proper stuff costs a fortune).

- **Hardboard**. A very dense, highly compressed, usually thin fibreboard, popular in construction work for protecting floors, cutting templates and furniture making. Also available as a 'peg board', perforated with small holes.

- **Laminated planks** of various timber species. Blocks or strips of real timber are finger jointed and glued together to make wide boards. Often engineered out of small pieces of timber making it very stable and resistant to distortion.

- **MDF** Medium Density Fibreboard. The new standard in 'hobby' boards. Used everywhere. Now even available faced with real wood, melamine, and even an exterior grade.

- **OSB** Oriented Strand Board. Made from wood shavings glued and compressed. Makes a stronger board than chipboard. Common for any non-face work in construction from sheathing and roofing to hoardings around building sites.

- **Composite boards**. Used in the manufacture of stuff like caravans etc. Multiple materials laminated together, (e.g. polystyrene with an aluminium skin bonded on one side and thin plywood on the other). Strong and lightweight but very expensive.

- **Technical boards**. Exterior grade plywood with a range of different non-slip surfaces, often in a grid or mesh pattern. Perfect for use in trailers, scaffold platforms and other walkways, outdoor furniture and play equipment.

383. Some Good Brick Glues

Otherwise known as mortar. You might not think of mortar as 'glue', but mortar is an adhesive and it does stick bricks or blocks together (although the philosophers argue that it simply holds them apart...).

In the trade, we call it, muck, mud, gobbo, pug etc. Mortar is usually soft sand mixed with a binder; either lime in the case of older buildings or nowadays, cement (or masonry cement) along with a few additives to slow down the setting reaction and make it workable.

Try scraping a mortar joint on your house. If it's buff coloured and scrapes out relatively easily (and it's an old house) it's a lime putty and sharp sand mix. If the mortar is greyer coloured and hard (and the house is post WII) then it's more likely to be a cement and soft sand mix.

Of course, there are many different mixes within these two broad types and the exact mix of the mortar you should use depends on two factors, the strength of the brick/stone units themselves and the severity of their exposure to the elements or weather.

First, it's important your new mortar is slightly weaker than the units in the wall, because this allows the (slightly softer) joints to absorb any gentle movement of the structure as it settles onto its foundation under its own weight.

If the mortar were stronger than the units in the wall, everything would be very rigid, and any movement would cause stress to build within the wall itself, cracking joints (zig zag cracks), and units alike (shear cracks).

Second, the mortar must be able to withstand many years of whatever the environment throws at it. Wind, rain, and freezing temperatures plus salt or other chemicals (acidic rain etc.). Ergo the mortar used to build a chimney in an exposed clifftop location in a cold climate needs to be much more durable than the mortar used to build a decorative fireplace in your lounge for example.

In addition to sand and a binder you'll need an additive in the form of a liquid plasticiser (never washing up liquid...). This improves the workability no end. Add the recommended amount of mortar plasticiser exactly to the following mixes and you'll end up with soooo smooth mortar it will roll off your tools beautifully.

The following mortar mix ratios (or multiples thereof) will cover most building situations...

- **1:2½** which is 1 lime putty (or bagged lime product) to 2½ sieved sharp sand (particle size from dust up to around a third of the average mortar joint height, e.g. Typically 0.1mm to 3mm).

Alternatively use a proprietary lime mortar blend from a specialist supplier of lime mortars for old masonry. 1:2½ is a general mix suitable for most old brickwork built with lime mortar under normal exposure conditions.

- **1:3** which is 1 cement to 3 building or bricklaying sand. Very strong mix, suitable for very hard materials such as blue bricks, concrete bricks or blocks or severe environmental conditions such as salty air, acid rain etc. Plus plasticiser.

- **1:4** which is 1 cement to 4 building or bricklaying sand. Strong mix suitable for engineering bricks or hard bricks in general including exposed conditions such as chimneys or garden walls or below ground masonry etc.

- **1:5** which is 1 cement to 5 building or bricklaying sand. Medium strength mix suitable for most bricks exposed to normal conditions above ground.

- **1:6** which is 1 cement to 6 building or bricklaying sand. Soft mix suitable for sheltered or protected masonry and indoor work such as internal blockwork.

  1:1:6 which is 1 cement, 1 lime and 6 building or bricklaying sand. A good general purpose, medium strength mix, for bricks, block, and stone under normal conditions.

  (You can add lime to the other ratios in this list too as it acts as a good plasticiser, improving workability.)

- **1:9** which is 1 cement to 9 building or bricklaying sand. A very weak mix, suitable for lightweight blocks and bedding items subject to some movement (needs to be a super accurate gauged mix).

The most important thing to remember when mixing your own mortar is to MEASURE each component of the ratio. i.e. make it a gauged mix.

If you throw it all in willy-nilly using a shovel, the actual mix ratio will be all over the place. No two mixes will be the same, different colour, different strength, different consistency, different durability. Don't do it. Use a small bucket, i.e. one bucket of cement, 6 buckets of sand for 1:6 ratio.

If all that seems like too much trouble, most DIY stores sell dry 'ready-mix' mortar in bags where you just need to add water. These are great for those smaller jobs on modern buildings as one bag mixes easily in a wheelbarrow with just a shovel. These are usually cement based though, so don't use them on period properties.

384. Some General Masonry Tips

- Watch your running length, each brick needs to sit exactly half over the brick below (in the most common half bond) allowing a little for the vertical, cross joint.

- Keep a close eye on the line position. If it moves out of position, it'll throw out your bricklaying too (flick the line and watch it vibrate, if it doesn't it means something is touching it and pushing it out).

- Finish off your mortar joints regularly with the tool of your choice (half round or bucket handle being the most common in the UK). Don't leave it too long before finishing them off (especially if it's hot) or it will be hard work and you'll get poorly finished joints (black lines).

- After jointing up (finishing the joints) and at the end of the day's work, give the bricks a very light brushing with a soft brush to give it a final flourish in the quality department.

- If you get mortar on the bricks wait until you're finished and then apply a special brick cleaner, (it's a type of acid), followed by a good rinsing (personally I don't like the idea of splashing acid around, but then I keep my brickwork clean...).

- In the summer time 'greedy', softer, bricks might need soaking with water a few minutes before laying to counter their extreme suction.

- Cover all your work down at the end of the day to protect it from the weather, especially if it's going to get cold or wet. Mortar fleece and polythene are great with a plank on top and bottom to stop it blowing off.

385. Some Good Concrete Mixes

These four mix ratios will cover most situations and they are comprised as follows...

- **1:1.5:2.5** which is one cement, 1.5 sand and 2.5 stone. (or **1:4** cement and all-in-ballast). Very strong mix suitable for reinforced concrete and padstones or areas needing great strength or water resistance etc. Similar to C35 RMC.

- **1:2:4** which is one cement, 2 sand and 4 stone (or **1:6** cement and all-in-ballast). Good general strength mix for slabs, paths, floors etc. Similar to C20 RMC.

- **1:2.5:5.5** which is one cement, 2.5 sand and 5.5 stone. (**1:8** cement and all-in-ballast). Slightly weaker mix good for foundations in good ground, fence posts, etc. Similar to C15 RMC.

- **1:3.5:6.5** lean mix which is one cement, 4 sand and 8 stone (**1:10** cement and all-in-ballast). Weak mix for cavity fill, soft spot infill, blinding, certain hard landscaping work etc. Similar to C7.5 RMC.

As with mixing mortar, the most important thing to remember when mixing concrete is to MEASURE each component of the ratio. i.e. make it a gauged mix. If you throw it all in willy-nilly using a shovel, the actual mix ratio will be correspondingly all over the place. No two mixes will be the same, different colour, different strength, different slump, different durability. Don't do it. Use a small bucket, i.e. one bucket of cement, 2

buckets of sand and 4 buckets of stones for 1:2:4.

386. Cure Your Concrete (and no, it's not sick)

Wet concrete contains a large amount of water which will evaporate as the concrete cures or dries. The slower this happens the better it is for the concrete. Rapid water loss compromises the final strength of the concrete i.e. it's weaker. Wind and warm weather will dry out concrete very quickly (especially slabs).

It is critical to slow down water loss by keeping it damp for a week (longer is even better). After the initial set, (which occurs after a few hours), concrete continues to strengthen and harden, reaching 90% or so after around a month, depending on the location and weather.

After this period concrete continues to harden but very slowly over many years. Old concrete is often very hard indeed.

Fortunately, it's easy to slow down this water loss. Once the concrete surface is firm (a few hours), cover it up with polythene and weigh down the edges (bricks, planks, sand bags etc.), to stop the wind getting underneath. Wetting underneath and/or on top of the polythene holds the polythene in place.

Keep an eye on the surface colour of the concrete under the sheet, it should look dark and wet, if it's light grey and dry, add more water quick.

HEALTH AND SAFETY

Ouch! (although most folks use other words in these situations, some also with four letters...). Arguably, when you work with tools and materials, small injuries are almost inevitable, because even the most careful and cautious folks will occasionally catch their hand on something, trap a finger or slip with a tool.

However, serious injuries are a different matter. You can reduce the risk significantly by adopting safe working practices, every time...no exceptions. Sorry to go on about this, but it's really important!

387. Understanding Risk and DIY

Remember you're literally gambling with your life (or other peoples), if you choose to...

- Succumb to pressure and cut corners to finish a job quickly.

- Work with the wrong tool for the job.

- Work without proper protective gear.

- Work on unsafe or inappropriate support/scaffolding.

- Use unfamiliar tools without studying and practicing first.

- Make any decision that ignores your personal safety.

- Make any decision that ignores the safety of others.

...because sooner or later, you will have an 'accident', I put quotes around the word accident because true accidents are rare, most 'accidents' are a result of a bad choice or a poor judgement call.

Risk is inherent in many things we do, but DIY is especially risky. Not only can you damage your home but yourself also.

There's no doubt that tackling some DIY jobs means using new and potentially dangerous tools or moving heavy materials plus difficult situations either in or on the ground or even at considerable height.

Even clearing up and removing rubbish, junk, or spoil or removing or dismantling... well, anything at all really entails risk.

These situations require specific safety measures as mistakes can easily be fatal. You must take this stuff seriously because your first mistake could also be your last...

388. You Are Everything!

Sweet I know, but you really are everything! So never forget the most important thing in your world is you. Everything and I mean everything else is unimportant compared to your health and safety. Because if you get hurt, injured or dead, you won't be able to finish the job and that will never do!

A true handy person always works safely, because injuries slow you down and might delay the start of the next fun project...

If you're reading this as a 'young un', i.e. someone under say 30 (ancient I know!) you might be scoffing at all this stuff. I'm as fit as a butcher's dog you might say, watch me bounce ping-pong balls off my abs.

But believe this. *What you do today, affects what you can do tomorrow.*

I know because I used to be that hero on the building site; running about on rooftops unsecured, abusing ladders and lifting what I now know to be insane weights; steel beams, oak beams, concrete lintels, timber etc. Not to mention thousands of tons of other smaller materials over the years, all by hand.

Stupid and definitely not clever. Ask my knees now, go on ask... Oh, I'm sorry, they can't hear you over the creaking, clicking and groans of pain...

Remember that human beings are not forklift trucks, (that's why we have forklift trucks...). If you repeatedly abuse something i.e. your body, it will eventually wear out, and 50 ain't that old, it's the new 40, hadn't you heard?

WARNING: Ignoring this advice may have serious consequences for your long-term health! When you're older and wiser and more experienced and more skilled, and (hopefully) wealthier, you'll still want to be active, so start the habit now, always work safe... every time.

Keeping your blood where it belongs then, let's expand on the most important tips to help you stay safe...

389. PPP: Proper Personal Protection

This equipment is mostly a no-brainer; you know this stuff, so use it okay?

- Avoid wearing lose clothing near rotary machines and don't wear any jewellery whilst working, even rings, (free!).

- Use safety glasses when using tools that could cause sparks or debris to fly, they are effective, and easy to use, there's no logical reason not to use them. Plus, they are as comfortable as sunglasses these days, gone are the hopeless misting goggles of yore, (very cheap).

- Wear gloves when handling materials and when using club hammers and cold chisels etc. to protect your hands (cheap). Gloves also prevent getting rough skin, which might snag stockings, either your own or someone else's, (priceless).

- Wear a good thick leather belt to support your back. Helpful if you have a lot of heavy lifting to do; some folks even swear by a weightlifter's belt to support a hard working back, (medium cost).

- Wear coveralls etc. when using chemicals or irritating stuff like insulation. Plus, they're handy against dirt too, (cheap).

- Hard hats, if there is a 'reasonable risk' of falling debris and always if there are people and/ or loose material above you, (cheap).

- Wear high visibility (Hi-Vis) clothing if working with others or in a busy location, (cheap).

- Wear a facemask when working in dusty conditions, with insulation materials or cutting treated timber etc. Disposables or even better, a proper filtered facemask, (cheap).

- Wear ear protection when using loud tools, tools in enclosed spaces or for any extended length of time. Tiny and cheap foam plugs as a minimum or better, proper over the head ear defenders, (cheap).

- Use steel toe capped boots if handling heavy stuff. Good ankle protection too, (medium cost).

- Having an accident and injuring yourself because you didn't bother with any of the above, (very, very expensive).

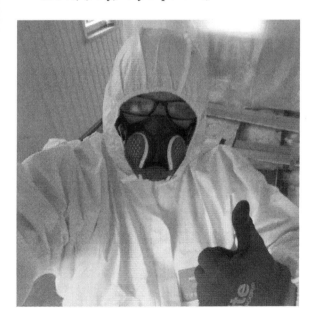

390. Take Your Time

Rushing about to finish quickly will eventually cause you to lose some skin or even some precious blood. Why? Because when you're rushing, safety concerns are not your first priority, getting the project finished is.

Working safely should always be uppermost in your mind, no matter how urgent the project is. Rushing to finish quickly could even finish you, it happens believe me, more often than you think.

I've 'only' seen one person die on the job and that's one too many, but I've seen plenty of stupid accidents, some of them my own.

Even if you only hurt yourself a little bit, you'll slow yourself down. This is a big problem for a professional. Most of the curses that fly when we injure ourselves are because our dumb mistake will hamper and slow us down for days afterwards, costing us time off work and money.

Also, ask yourself, who's benefiting from your risk taking? Mostly it's someone else! If your other half (or the client if it's your own business,) is complaining about how long a job is taking, remind them that top quality work always takes a little longer, think Rolls Royce not Trabant!

391. DIY Can Make You Fit (YMMV!)

Make DIY be a part of your keep fit regime by keeping you active. Keep in mind your current level of fitness though, because some DIY tasks are very strenuous.

You wouldn't embark on a 10-mile run if you'd only ever done 2-mile walks, would you? No, so don't make the first project a biggie in the garden. Like everything else we've looked in this book, start small and work your way up, slowly.

392. Poor Judgement or Decisions

Making a poor judgement call could cause an accident. But every decision you make related to safety must be an informed one; a conscious one.

Maybe one day you're pressed for time, and you want to take a 'short cut'; but always,

always ask yourself, what are the implications? What are the consequences?

Because if you misjudged the risk or danger, or played them down, *just because you were pressed for time*. Then your decision could, and probably would, lead to an accident.

For example, at the town dump, if you get pierced by a nail sticking out of a piece of skirting board, it's because at some point you made the decision to leave the nails sticking out when you took the skirting board off the wall (to save a few seconds).

And that is a very mild example, believe me, I've seen much, much worse...

393. Using the Wrong Tool for the Job

I know it's a nuisance when you're working in the attic and you need yet another tool from the shed/car/downstairs/etc.; but reaching for the wrong tool can cost you dearly in terms of blood or damage to the workpiece.

Before you start up the stairs, out into the garden or head for the scaffold with your bucket of tools, take a moment, close your eyes if you need to, and conjure up a mental image of the task in hand. Picture yourself doing the work and what tools you need. Mentally walk through it.

Do you have everything you might need in your bucket?

The right tool for the right job
Every time!

394. Thinking, It'll Only Take a Minute

That tiny job to put one screw in, or push something into place, is not an excuse to take short cuts with your safety. It only takes a fraction of a second to slip, fall, cut, or catch yourself.

The length of the job is never an excuse to take short cuts with safe working practices.

395. Using the Wrong Materials or Fixings

Always make the extra effort to use the right thing for the job you're doing. A nail will only do a screws job for so long before it fails. If the job calls for specific fixings, use them. When fixings fail, things fall apart and someone might get hurt, not to mention your pride...

Always follow the manufacturer's instructions. For example, if the instructions say the glue isn't water resistant, don't expect it to last very long if you use it outside. Oh, and don't build a boat with interior grade plywood, even if you paint it well, (and yes, I know the proper marine ply is expensive) unless you're a really good swimmer etc...

396. Thinking, a Ladder is Fine

According to the World Health Organisation (WHO), 424,000 people die from falling, plus another 37.3 million falls are severe enough to need medical attention (globally). Every... single... year. This makes falling the second biggest cause of accidental death after motoring accidents.

If you don't want to join them, always use proper scaffolding with safety rails when doing anything at any kind of height i.e. over 2m (6′ or so.) Using a platform will enable you to work much quicker compared with working off a ladder because you'll have more space and a much better reach.

When I first started out, I took crazy risks on ladders because I thought hiring scaffolding was expensive. I soon realised the only person benefitting was my customer as I was billing for labour, materials, and access equipment 'as used'.

Essentially, I risked my life for nothing. If you can't afford to do the job with safe access, then forget it, let the darn thing fall down. You simply can't risk your life to work on your house.

397. Thinking It Won't Happen to Me...

Don't tell me you weren't thinking that because I know you were (because everyone does).

No one gets up in the morning with the intention of having an accident, no one, ever. You're probably thinking, 'Oh, I'll be alright, it wouldn't happen to me because I know what I'm doing, I'm careful, I know what's an acceptable risk.'

Come on admit it, you're thinking those guys must have been a tiny bit dumb to have an accident; you've seen the YouTube videos, right?

Well, maybe that's true, but more likely they were regular guys getting on with the job thinking, 'I'll be alright, it won't happen to me because I know what I am doing, I'm careful'... just... like... you...

398. First Aid Kit

If you're not used to working with your hands, the concept of getting hurt and seeing yourself bleed might come as a bit of a shock the first time.

Be prepared, put together a simple first aid kit before you start. No need to buy anything fancy. If you need anything fancy, then arguably you should be calling for an ambulance to take you to the hospital...

This is what I keep in my own kits, (car, home and at work... and yes, that's three kits!).

- **Antiseptic wipes and sprays** (ouch, okay they hurt a bit, but think about the how dirty that wound is. It's important to avoid infection.

- **Pair of round nose medical scissors** for cutting bandages etc. and for cutting clothing from more serious injuries.

- **A pair of good tweezers** and a medium size sewing needle (for splinters) Wipe everything with an antiseptic wipe first.

- **Capsules of sterile water**. Twist off the top to rinse wounds. For debris in the eye, pierce the top with needle and gently squeeze capsule and use the thin stream to rinse debris out of the eye.

- **Plasters** to protect small damage (minor blood loss). Personally, I don't use them for cuts as the non-sticky part/pad allows the cut to open and close as you move around. In most cases, I like to 'stitch' a cut closed with tape or steri-strips, this closes the cut and keeps it closed allowing the body to repair the damage (always clean first).

- **Thin adhesive tape or 'steri-strips'** (butterfly stitches) for medium size cuts (medium blood loss). Close wound and stick them straight across the cut, spaced at around 1cm ($^3/_8''$) intervals (after cleaning thoroughly of course).

- **Small compress pads** for medium cuts or skin damage (serious, scary looking blood loss)

- **Medium compress pads** for large damage (very serious, very scary looking blood loss)

- **Large compress pads** plus roll and triangular bandages for serious damage (call an ambulance kind of blood loss!)

- **Roll of 25mm (1") adhesive tape** to hold compress pads in place.

- **A proper, first aid bag**, clearly marked and accessible to put it all in.

I add a few extra things to my car first aid kit, like a blanket, disposable gloves, a one-way resuscitation valve and a torch with spare batteries.

The theory is that the better the first aid kit, the less likely you are to need one!

On a lighter note...
Splinters.

You're going to get them for sure, and rather than digging around blindly with blunt tools, get yourself a jeweller's loupe or magnifier or glasses.

They miraculously turn that miniscule, annoying sliver of wood (or metal, glass, thorn etc.) into a massive tree trunk, which you can gently and much less painfully negotiate out, using a clean needle and a pair of tweezers.

20x magnification jewellers loupe

Oh, and don't worry, you'll get really good at 'operating' on yourself...

And lastly; always keep your first aid kit easily accessible. Don't forget it might not be you who needs to find it.

It might be you lying on the floor, bleeding out, or unconscious; so you'd better hope whoever finds you, can also find your first aid kit and that it has what you need...

Jeeze, tough love huh!

Right, as they say in the old cartoons

"That's all folks!"

END NOTES

How did you get on, what do you think?
Are you inspired to have a go at DIY?

It's taken me well over 30 years working on the tools to gain enough experience to write this book, that's over 50,000 hours. Phew. Still it'll only take you a few minutes to leave a review won't it. *wink*, *wink*...

If you think this book will help others,
I'd love it if you'd leave a review for me...

Amazon.co.uk **author.to/iananderson**

amazon.com/author/iananderson

goodreads.com/ian-anderson

For insults, typos you noticed, suggestions for revisions or general mudslinging, or if you want an address to send chocolate to, I'll look forward to hearing from you in person via email at ian@handycrowd.com ......

But wait, don't get your coat just yet, there is still a little more stuff to come in the appendix... (and just when you thought you'd finished...)

As you were...

APPENDIX (FOR MORE TIPS!)

Here are some online resources I've personally found useful. But please bear in mind that things change, and links break all the time... (let me know if you hit a broken link or want to suggest a new one).

Some of the links are very people 'unfriendly' so to save your poor typing fingers, I've copied these pages and put the links online here: handycrowd.com/links so you can just click them... you're welcome!

BUILDING RELATED TOPICS

Askjeff.co.uk: Popular newspaper columnist, builder by trade, now teaching and writing to help others better look after their homes.

Brick.org.uk: UK based brick resource.

British-gypsum.com: Great installation guides for drywall and plasters in the UK.

Calderlead.co.uk/wp-content/uploads/2011/07/Calder-Guide-to-Good-Lead-work.pdf: For a great leadwork guide.

Diydoctor.org.uk: Popular place for DIY information and advice articles plus a forum.

Diynot.com: DIY encyclopaedia and active forum covering a wide range of topics.

Gobrick.com: USA based brick resource.

Gov.uk/government/uploads/system/uploads/attach-ment_data/file/516238/160413_Householder_Technical_Guidance.pdf: Permitted development notes in the UK.

Homebuilding.co.uk: Physical magazine with an online presence. Lots of how to and tips articles.

Idostuff.co.uk: Informal DIY advice & tips.

Ihbconline.co.uk/caring: Great resource for older homes from The Institute of Historic Building Conservation, accessed via the little 'hamburger' icon in the top left-hand corner.

Leadsheetassociation.org.uk: All you need to know to make the most out of lead as a good, long lasting building material.

Lime.org.uk: All about lime and its proper use.

Nhbc.co.uk: National House Building Council who are responsible for new housing standards in the UK.

Nps.gov/tps/how-to-preserve/briefs/2-repoint-mortar-joints.htm: How to re-point the mortar joints on your house using the correct materials.

Periodliving.co.uk: Magazine based DIY advice with an old house flavour.

Planningportal.co.uk: Advice and procedures related to UK planning and building regulations

Pointmaster.co.uk: Pumps mortar into empty joints in brick/paving via a nozzle.

Ultimatehandyman.co.uk: Over 50,000 pages of DIY info and an active forum.

Wickes.co.uk: UK based home DIY supplier.

En.wikipedia.org/wiki/Electrical_wiring: To fully understand just how ridiculously complex cable colours are in domestic wiring.

COMPUTER RELATED TOPICS

Dropbox.com: Dropbox automatically saves your stuff to a server in the 'cloud'. First 2GB free.

Dummies.com: Excerpts from the Dummies guide books (there are other topics too).

Fixyourownprinter.com: How to fix your own printer (printers have all sorts of hidden menus you can exploit for repairs...).

Help.lockergnome.com: A great online forum about computer problems.

Howtogeek.com: Brilliant place to get help with computer problems.

Onedrive.live.com: Like Dropbox, OneDrive is a cloud-based storage facility from Microsoft with first 5GB free.

Pcworld.com: Lots of how to articles and advice.

Primopdf.com: The No1 free PDF converter. Simple to convert documents to PDF format for easy and safe distribution.

Processlibrary.com: The place to go to find out what computer process is running.

Speedtest.net: Check your internet connection speeds, uploads and downloads, (contact your provider for not keeping their promise!)

Techguy.org: Free tech support...heaven! Although they won't say no to a small donation.

Technibble.com: A vibrant community of Computer Technicians sharing their knowledge with each other and you.

Techrepublic.com: Top resource for the IT trade, lots of useful tips and tweaks.

Thewindowsclub.com: Large community for windows support with active forum and many useful articles to help you.

FUN STUFF

Climbingarborist.com: Great tree climbing resource from Dan Holiday a trained arborist.

Craftster.org: Online community where people share hip, offbeat, crafty projects. 'No tea cosies without irony' is the tag line...

Duckworksbbs.com/plans/gavin/mouse: Free plans to build a mouse boat, one of the simplest boats to build in the world.

Fornobravo.com/pompeii_oven: Free plans to build a wood fired pizza oven!

For-wild.org: Plans to build an Aldo Leopold bench, probably the easiest cool looking bench to build there is.

Glen-L.com: The holy grail for home boat builders!

Lifehacker.com: Tips to get you through life with a twist of humour and the faintly ridiculous!

Stormdrane.blogspot.com: For anything you need to make out of paracord, surely one of the most useful materials.

Treehousesupplies.com: Inspiration, for building that tree house you always wanted?

Treetopbuilders.net: More treehouses!

Woodenboat.com: Great help for anyone contemplating building or owning a wooden boat. New or old.

Ziplinegear.com/manual: Everything you need to know about building the kids a Zip line or flying fox.

GENERAL TOPICS

About.com: 'Need. Know. Accomplish.' Say the people at about.com, a huge online resource of practical information.

Blog.makezine.com: Community of resourceful people who undertake amazing projects.

Bongous.com: Gives you an address in the USA for delivery purposes, (if your supplier doesn't ship internationally) Bongo then forwards it to you for a small fee plus actual delivery cost.

Justanswer.com: A paid 'ask an expert' service. Over 100 categories and you don't pay until they have answered to your satisfaction.

Handycrowd.com: Me, of course! Companion to this book. Come in, I'll go and put the kettle on...

Multimedia.3m.com/mws/media/3724890/adhesives-and-tapes-design-guide.pdf: Hundreds of 3M bonding solutions PDF.

Popularmechanics.com: Great general practical info on a wide range of topics. Been around a long time!

Selfsufficientish.com: Urban homesteading on a budget. Good advice on making stuff and saving money.

Wikipedia.org: Background reading for pretty much everything!

Youtube.com/watch?v=f2O6mQkFiiw: Learn what happens what happens to your brain when you practice.

MAINTENANCE AND REPAIR RELATED TOPICS

Buildingconservation.com: Conservation information about methods, products, and services for historic buildings.

Cadw.wales.gov.uk/historicenvironment: Information about looking after old buildings and conservation in general. Available from the Welsh Gov.at

Ereplacementparts.com: Great place to find parts and repair advice with videos, forum, and active Facebook resources.

Howtomendit.com: Wide ranging 'How To' site.

Ifixit.com: Free online repair manual.

maintenancematterswales.org: Advice about looking after an older home including sections on planning your maintenance properly and keeping records. From the Welsh Gov.

PLASTIC RELATED TOPICS

info.craftechind.com/download-the-full-guide-to-gluing-plastics: Guide to gluing plastics.

Microfluidics.cnsi.ucsb.edu/processing/237471_LT2197_Plastic_Guide_v6_LR7911911.pdf. Loctite, a guide to binding the 30 most common plastics.

Nerfhaven.com: Intro to solvent welding plastics. Available at Nerfhaven.com/forums/topic/18527-intro-to-solvent-welding-plastic

Polyvance.com/identify.php: Best plastic identification and how to repair plastic table on the net.

Weldguru.com/plasticrepair.html: Learn how to weld plastics.

TIMBER RELATED TOPICS

Finewoodworking.com: Leading magazine and TV based info.

Nzffa.org.nz/specialty-timber-market/glossary-of-timber-terms/ Great list of all the terms used in timber production.

Salford.gov.uk/media/385493/inform-insect-attack.pdf: Great introduction to wood boring insect attacks.

Timberworkforums.com: Ozzie based timberwork forum with loads of good advice and a friendly crowd.

TOOLS AND HARDWARE RELATED TOPICS

Boltdepot.com: Lots of fastener related information.

Custompartnet.com/drill-size-chart: Chart for HSS drill bit sizes by gauge, inch, and metric.

Heinnie.com: Because every handy person needs a good, reliable knife. Biggest and best.

Rawlplug.co.uk/downloads: Detailed instructions on using anchors.

Screwfix.com: A UK supplier of building materials with a great multi trade forum with many professionals and a few nuts!

TooledUp.com: UK based supplier of tools and equipment.

VEHICLE RELATED TOPICS

Autorepair.about.com: Simple car maintenance advice and tutorials.

Autotrader.co.uk: Reviews are great for finding potential problems with your car.

Fuelly.com: Track your fuel consumption because increased consumption is an early warning that your motor needs a tune up.

Obd-codes.com: On board, diagnostic stuff, OBD2 or OBDII to work out what fault codes mean on your car.

Parkers.co.uk/cars/reviews: Reviews are great for finding potential problems with your car.

Theaa.com/motoring-advice: Motoring related advice on a wider range of topics.

Usedcarexpert.co.uk: Used car experts for general info etc.

Wisebuyers.co.uk: First call for car related reviews, prices, and specifications.

GETTING IN TOUCH

Please remember you're not alone. If you have questions, suggestions, or want to point out spelling mistakes or you just want to tell me about a better way. Please feel free to get in touch and I'll get back to you ......

CONTACT DETAILS

I'm happy to stand behind this book (and not only to avoid any eggs!) Of course, if the book makes the bestseller lists, I'll be far too busy on my boat to talk to you personally, but in that case, I promise I'll have one of my minions handle your enquiry...

For the foreseeable future however, I'd be delighted to hear from you. I'm always open to feedback and I'd love to read any constructive criticism you might have. If you're a spammer though, or overly rude, I'll have my men track you down...

You can email me at ian@handycrowd.com, or catch up with me on most flavours of social media. Just search for 'handycrowd' at Facebook, Twitter, Pinterest, or LinkedIn

COMPANION WEBSITE

You'll also find me pottering about on handycrowd.com where I'll be writing more 'how to' articles and answering your emails or comments.
Come on in, I'll go and put the kettle on!

NEWSLETTER

You can also register for updates and newsletters and I promise not to abuse your email address. I'll only write when there's something interesting or useful for you, Christmas's, and birthdays etc...

ABOUT THE AUTHOR

Hang on a sec. I'm not going to write this in the third person, because that's just silly, right?

I'm Ian Anderson, an English builder and I've been self-employed since the tender age of 18. I was awarded a silver trowel at college for my skills with a trowel, as well as the silver medal, first prize for surveying and levelling, I'm now a Licentiate member of the City and Guilds Institute of London.

I've built new houses, extensions, restored period houses using lime mortars, underpinned ancient foundations, and restored centuries old roofing, as well as carrying out routine repairs and maintenance work on a variety of properties in the UK.

I'm also a keen home mechanic and love classic cars. Oh, and I love recycling and repurposing stuff, especially pallets, my standard 'go-to' resource.

I'm a keen humanitarian and have lived and worked in various East African countries. In Uganda, I taught local artisans and built health units in remote rural areas, plus the restoration of a couple of hospitals. I also helped to set up projects in Rwanda as part of a British Conservative Party initiative by David Cameron for his international development team under Andrew Mitchell MP (project Umubano).

Later I took a Master of Science degree in Trauma and Disaster Management from the University of Lincoln in the UK, mostly to better help me understand my experiences working in East Africa, but also because the topic interests me and it looked a lot of fun (and indeed it was!).

To balance things out I was a househusband or 'Mr Mom' for a couple of years; looking after 3 acres of wild New Zealand scrub, two chickens and of course my Norwegian wife, and two fantastic children.

I'm a 'try anything' handyman (or should that be 'repairperson' these days?) and it's my goal to learn something new every day. This I find very easy to do, as I'm writing, inventing, developing products and webmastering (all self-taught of course), close to the beach in Norway with, fortunately the same wife, even bigger kids, and even more crazy chickens. And yes, of course, the days are never long enough...

Stay well, and I wish you well in all your own endeavours.

Index

Printed in Great Britain
by Amazon